Unriddling
Our Times

Also by Os Guinness

The American Hour: A Time of Reckoning and the Once and Future Role of Faith

The Call: Finding and Fulfilling the Central Purpose of Your Life

Character Counts: Leadership Qualities in Washington, Wilberforce, Lincoln, and Solzhenitsyn

Dining with the Devil: The Megachurch Movement Flirts with Modernity

The Dust of Death: The Sixties Counterculture and How It Changed America Forever

Fit Bodies, Fat Minds: Why Evangelicals Don't Think and What to Do about It

God in the Dark: The Assurance of Faith Beyond a Shadow of Doubt

Invitation to the Classics, coeditor

Unriddling Our Times

REFLECTIONS ON THE GATHERING CULTURAL CRISIS

OS GUINNESS

EDITOR

Baker Books

A Division of Baker Book House Co
Grand Rapids, Michigan 49516

Published by Baker Books
a division of Baker Book House Company
P.O. Box 6287, Grand Rapids, MI 49516-6287

Printed in the United States of America

Library of Congress Cataloging-in-Publication Data

Unriddling our times : reflections on the gathering cultural crisis / Os Guinness, editor.
    p.   cm.
ISBN 0-8010-5981-X
    1. Christian ethics—United States. 2. United States—Moral conditions. I. Guinness, Os.
BJ1275.U57 1999
270.8′29—dc21   99-32958

"Telling Truth to Kings" by Reinhold Schneider is from *Imperial Mission (Las Casas vor Karl V.)* by Reinhold Schneider, translated by Walter Oden. Copyright © 1948 by The Gresham Press. Reprinted by permission of the Reinhold Schneider Association of Germany.

"One Word of Truth: A Portrait of Aleksandr Solzhenitsyn" by David Aikman is adapted from *Great Souls: Six Who Changed Their Century* by David Aikman, copyright 1998, Word Publishing, Nashville, Tennessee. All rights reserved.

"The Lottery" from THE LOTTERY AND OTHER STORIES by Shirley Jackson. Copyright © 1948, 1949 by Shirley Jackson. Copyright renewed 1976, 1977 by Laurence Hyman, Barry Hyman, Mrs. Sarah Webster, and Mrs. Joanne Schnurer. Reprinted by permission of Farrar, Straus and Giroux, L.I.C., New York, and Robinson Publishing Ltd., London.

"Suspending Moral Judgment: Students Who Refuse to Condemn the Unthinkable," by Kay Haugaard, *The Chronicle of Higher Education*, 27 June 1997, reprinted as "The Lottery Revisited" with permission of the author.

For information about academic books, resources for Christian leaders, and all new releases available from Baker Book House, visit our web site:
http://www.bakerbooks.com

Contents

Introduction

OS GUINNESS

Prisoner 174517 was thirsty. Seeing a fat icicle hanging just outside his hut in the Auschwitz extermination camp, he reached out the window and broke it off hoping to quench his thirst. But before he could get it to his mouth, a guard snatched it out of his hands and dashed it to pieces on the filthy ground.

"Why?" the prisoner burst out instinctively.

"Here, there is no why," the guard answered with brutal finality.

That, for Primo Levi, the Italian Jewish scientist and writer, was the essence of the death camps—places not only of unchallengeable arbitrary authority but of absolute evil that defied all explanation. In the face of such evil, explanations born of psychology, sociology, and economics were pathetic in their inadequacy. One could only shoulder the weight of such an experience and bear witness to the world. "Never again" was too confident an assertion. "You never know" was the needed refrain.

Yet despite the horror, Levi gave the impression that he had survived the poison of Auschwitz and come to terms with his nightmarish experience. One of only three returning survivors of the 650 Italian Jews transported to Poland in 1944, he eventually married, had children, wrote books, won literary prizes, and lived a full life—but always around the core mission of serving as a witness to the truth, a guardian of the memory.

It was therefore a terrible shock to many when more than forty years later, on April 11, 1987, Primo Levi plunged to his death down the stairwell of the house in which he lived. Feeling the burden of witnessing, the guilt of surviving, the horror of revisionist denials of the camps, the weariness of repeating the same things, and even the anxiety of seeing his own memories fade, he joined the long, sad list of the victims of the Nazi hell who took their own lives.

Levi's mounting depression in the last weeks of his life was known to his family and friends. Significantly, in his last interview, he begged the questioning journalist not to consider him a prophet: "Prophets are the plague of today, and perhaps of all time, because it is impossible to tell a true prophet from a false one." In the same vein he had said earlier, "All prophets are false. I don't believe in prophets, even though I come from a heritage of prophets . . ."

Prophets "the plague of all time"? Levi was an atheist, and he had been to hell on earth and back. So his dismissal of the prophets is therefore understandable, though sad, for the strong line of Hebrew prophets is not only a defining feature of his people's heritage but one of the richest Jewish gifts to the history of the world. Elijah, Elisha, Isaiah, Jeremiah, Amos, Hosea, and many others—each was a hero of the moral word whose "Thus says the Lord" shattered the status quo of his day and opened up perspectives on God's truth, justice, and peace that restored the world or moved it forward through a transcendent point of leverage.

If ever a generation needed a prophetic word, it is ours. Words, words, words—we are assaulted from all sides by words, but we are starved for a word from God. Blaring, blasting, hectoring, seducing, words come at us from all sides today—on billboards, bumper stickers, newspapers, television, and junk mail. But few modern words are decisive; they do not make things happen. Most are only accessories to images and accomplices to sales. And almost none— including sermons—bear any trace of a transcendent source or the sign of a wind from heaven. Prophets tear through social complacency and moral rottenness like bolts of lightning. But such occurrences are rare today as modern people sleep untroubled beneath a million lightning rods.

Doubtless, like Levi, we are right to be wary of false prophets, for the modern parade of counterfeits is as long as the list of true ones is short. Pundits from the chattering class with their automatic Olympian perspectives on everything, futurists with grandiose spiritual or secular scenarios for every possible outcome, marketers with "all-new, must-see" solutions and programs for every problem—the list of the prophetic-sounding is long but, in the end, flatters only to deceive. As Winston Churchill quipped, "The main qualification for political office is the ability to foretell what is going to happen tomorrow, next week, next month and next year. And to have the ability afterward to say why it didn't."

Historian Daniel Boorstin has written that our modern capacity for instant, total information has produced "homo up-to-datum," but homo up-to-datum is a dunce. People careless about such deceptions should consider the fate of the false prophets in Dante's Inferno (Canto XX). Having falsely pretended to see into the future, they are punished by having their heads turned backward so that they can see only behind them as they walk. Never able to see ahead of them in time, they are now unable to see ahead of them in space either. Far better the modesty of Churchill: "It is always wise to look ahead, but difficult to look farther than you can see."

Doubtless too, we might not welcome a true prophet if one appeared, nor find it comfortable to be one, if so called. Jeremiah had good reason to be called the weeping prophet, and Aleksandr Solzhenitsyn's granite resolve is easier to admire from a distance than to copy. Only the person who has undergone wilderness years, Churchill observed, has the "psychic dynamite" by which the prophet is made.

But when all is said and done we moderns are not let off the hook. The contemporary obsession "to know in order to predict in order to control" may only lead to information junkies, web-surfing trivial pursuit players, and navel-contemplating trendspotters. But for Jews and Christians at least, the answer is not to swing to the other extreme of complacency and isolation. The way forward lies in rejecting the current preoccupation with "know yourself" and insisting that the alternative saying, "know your moment," be taken in a biblical direction. The answer lies in the challenge of making sense of our situation by reading the signs of the times and assessing the significance of the moment.

As I read the Bible, and especially the teaching of Jesus in the Gospel of Luke, this challenge of interpreting the significance of the moment is the responsibility of all followers of Christ, not just some. We might distinguish capital-P "Prophets" from small-p "prophets." The former are those who have heard a direct, explicit, supernatural word from God and can legitimately say, "Thus says the Lord." The latter are those who interpret their life and times from a biblical perspective, and therefore, "read the signs of the times" with greater or lesser skill, never presuming the divine authority and infallibility of "Thus says the Lord." In this second and more modest sense we are all to be prophets—interpreting events from the perspective of faith and under the aspect of eternity, and always with an eye to what we should *do*, not simply know.

To be sure, if God has not spoken to us directly and explicitly, we must not confuse ourselves with capital-P prophets and presume to give our views the status of "Thus says the Lord." However boldly or bluntly we speak, the unspoken assumption is always, "This is how I see it as a person of faith." Neither as speakers nor as listeners can we say, "Thus says the Lord," unless it is truly so.

Put differently, our best attempts to read the signs of the times are finite and fallible, so we must always be modest and open to correction. History in its fullest sense is beyond our reach. But by staying aware of the enormous plane on which it is enacted and the only perspective—faith—in which it will ever make sense, we can give a responsible account of ourselves in our own special moment in time. Only the vantage point of the world's last day will disclose the full secrets of our own little day, but by seeing what we can of the present under God, we rise most responsibly to the challenge of seeing—and carrying out—God's purpose in our time.

What follows in this book is a series of readings, each with an introduction designed to encourage such reflection on where we are today. Each is only an example, and such assessments could be made of a hundred similar issues. As I said, I do not claim the mantle of a prophet in the capital-P sense. Nor, obviously, am I infallible. But like many in an earlier generation, I was encouraged to pick up the challenge of reading the signs of the times soon after I came to faith and have practiced it for over thirty years.

I have long argued, among other things, that the present period in the United States is "the American hour," a *kairos*-like moment of opportunity and challenge at the climax of the American century. Also that the root of the crisis is not in America's political order or economic order but in her cultural order—the world of churches, synagogues, families, schools, colleges, the press and media, arts and entertainment. Also that the response of the religious right to the crisis is as much a problem as a solution and needs to be redirected before it is too late.

11

This is not the place to rehearse or justify such claims, which are the burden of my book *The American Hour: A Time of Reckoning and the Once and Future Role of Faith.* Events in the years since that book was written have intensified these convictions immeasurably. But it is only fair to add that the number of those who disagree has mounted too. Indeed, with the good times rolling as the new millennium begins, many now claim that American culture is in rude good health. "On the eve of the new century," one writer puts it, "there is no escaping the good news."

Who is correct? We cannot both be. Let time and history tell. False prophets are the devil's compliment to true prophets, and many faulty readings are the price of some accurate ones. They should spur, not deter, us toward ever better readings of our times. But as almost all can agree, the stakes are momentous.

"How long will the American republic last?" That question was put to James Russell Lowell, American diplomat and poet, by a French statesman in the nineteenth century. He replied, "As long as the ideas of the men who founded it remain dominant."

Unquestionably, no generation of Americans has treated the framers' ideas as more alien than this one, and the consequences are easy to see. But is there a gathering cultural crisis as this book claims? Unlike storms, earthquakes, and other forces of nature, the rise and fall of nations is never deterministic. Human initiative and divine sovereignty are always decisive. Cultural crises may therefore build up but pass.

But when it becomes evident that America's current condition puts her solidly in one of history's classic "storm corridors," it would be prudent, to say the least, to be on the watch as the storm signs mount. For Christians to take refuge in the coward's comfort of being right posthumously is for us to "miss our moment," and there is no mistaking what Jesus thought of that. Responsible "unriddling" of the signs of the times is an urgent requirement of our day.

one

An Unheeded Messenger

OS GUINNESS

One of the most haunting figures in history is that of the unheeded messenger. Two such messengers in ancient times—Jeremiah and John the Baptist—have left their hallmark on the genre of public warnings. Every time we speak of a "jeremiad" we tip our caps to the weeping prophet, and we pay a belated compliment to the wild man of Judea whenever we talk of "a voice crying in the wilderness." But our modern use of these expressions also underscores why these messengers went unheeded. The jeremiad has become an art form of denunciation and lament—no longer taken factually as an item on the evening news. A "voice crying in the wilderness" is often spoken of as best left there—uncouth and not to be heeded.

In our own generation the figure of the unheeded messenger was well represented by Aleksandr Solzhenitsyn as he spoke at the Harvard commencement in 1978. But unquestionably the twentieth century's greatest example was Winston Churchill during his "wilderness years" in the 1930s. Farsighted, alone, somber, and indefatigable, he was appalled by what he called the "mush, slush, and gush" of a pacifist-dreaming Britain, a corrupt and divided France, and a remote and indifferent America. These countries were being led or lulled into oblivion before the menace of a rapidly rearming Germany.

In 1936, when the Stanley Baldwin government called for a review of the situation, Churchill commented acidly, "Anyone can see what the position is. The Government simply cannot make up their mind, or they cannot get the Prime Minister to make up his mind. So they go on in a strange paradox, decided only to be undecided, resolved to be irresolute, adamant for drift, solid for fluidity, all powerful to be impotent." The sleepwalking democracies with their "leaderless confusion" were unwittingly preparing more years "for the locusts to eat." Or as Churchill muttered at London's Savoy Hotel as the sounds of merriment surrounding the celebration of the Munich agreement reached him, "These poor people! They little know what they will have to face."

Two hundred years earlier in the English-speaking world, the unheeded messenger was Edmund Burke. Revered today for his profound political philosophy and high oratory, he was more often on the losing side during his lifetime. Indeed, he was roused to greatness by the momentous battles of his day—on behalf of conciliation with the American colonies, against the domestic power of George III, against the Jacobinism of the French Revolution, and in his prosecution of Warren Hastings.

The impeachment of Warren Hastings for corruption and injustice in British India occupied Burke for sixteen long years. His closing speech in the case alone lasted nine full days. But the outcome was failure. Hastings was acquitted, and Burke commented on those years saying, "I labored with the most assiduity and met with the least success." His fellow Whig leader Charles James Fox perfectly described one aspect of unheeded messengers: "Well! Burke is right—but Burke is often right, only he is right too soon."

A Dog That Barked

This chapter uncovers the magnificent voice of an unheeded messenger from outside the English-speaking world who deserves far wider recognition and honor. *Las Casas Before Charles V* is the greatest novel by Reinhold Schneider, one of the leading exponents of the German literary resistance to Nazism. In a 1945 survey of German culture during the Third Reich, the BBC World Service recognized Reinhold Schneider's prophetic stature when they described him as "the voice of one crying in the wilderness."

Reinhold Schneider was born in Baden-Baden in southwest Germany in 1903. His father was a Protestant hotel owner, but Schneider was raised a Catholic by his devout mother. After school he studied agriculture but abandoned this field to work for an art dealer in Dresden. There he was able to travel widely—to Portugal, Spain, France, Italy, England, and Scandinavia. And on two visits to England in 1934 and 1935, he had an experience that changed his life and reinforced his decision to resist Hitler by staying inside Germany rather than going into exile. "As I was trying to comprehend English history," he wrote later in his autobiography, "Christ stood all around me as Power." The experience, he said, inspired him with the daring to investigate the meaning of history and the question of humankind from the perspective of faith.

Schneider was already a writer rediscovering the genre of the carefully researched historical novel. But it was his newly awakened faith that gave him the depth of perspective and sense of calling that fueled his resistance to the Nazis. His earlier novel, *The Hohenzollern,* was finished in 1933 as the SS platoons marched down the street in front of his house in Potsdam. The Nazis were quick to recognize him as a threat. His writings were censored at first, then banned altogether in 1941. After the ban he wrote mostly poetry, essays, and biblical exposition. These later works were printed clandestinely and some reached a circulation of half a million. In 1944, he was charged with high treason by Reichsminister Martin Bormann but escaped the fate of such others as Dietrich Bonhoeffer because of the chaos of the last days of fighting.

"Telling Truth to Kings" is excerpted from *Las Casas Before Charles V,* first written in 1937 (and later somewhat misleadingly titled in English *Imperial Mission*). On the surface, the novel is about the atrocities of the Spanish conquistadores in the New World, but discerning readers knew well that Schneider was condemning the persecution of the Jews and the crimes committed in the Nazi concentration camps in the 1930s. The book was actually published in 1938, only a few months before "Crystal Night," when the Nazi storm troopers looted and burned Jewish shops and property. Through the story of Spain, Schneider was directly challenging the German understanding of Germany's character and destiny.

When Schneider was told of Dachau and other concentration camps in 1934, he wrote a short story, "The Comforter," which foreshadowed the heroic resistance to come. He wrote of the story's protagonist, Friedrich von Spee: "The authorities and judges might take it amiss or not—he did not want to be found among the number of those who are rejected by the prophet because they are dumb dogs that cannot bark."

This last powerful sentence of Schneider's refers to Isaiah 56:10 and describes his own life of resistance. Clearly he himself was no "dumb dog." Furiously, repeatedly, and at the risk of his own life, he barked his warnings to his nation's leaders. The warnings went unheeded, but no one could blame the watchdog.

The Untimeliness of the Timely

History's unheeded messengers have varied widely in both outcome and temperament. Some lived to see their vindication, some did not. Winston Churchill, aristocratic, cigar-chomping, and ebullient, is a far cry from John the Baptist, traditionally seen as wild-eyed and dining on locusts and honey. But despite such differences, common virtues emerge: discernment of the times, courage to repudiate powerful interests and fashion, perseverance in the face of daunting odds, seasoned wisdom born of a sense of history and their nation's place in it, and—supremely with the great Hebrew prophets—a ring of conviction in their message born of its transcendent source.

Despite history's vindication of these messengers, our own generation seems heedless of such warnings. For many people, the present is no time to pay attention to alarms—the good times are rolling and they are taken as automatic disproof of the need for the slightest concern. For others, especially thought-leaders and opinion-shapers, tone deafness about faith means they cannot pick up on themes critical to the nation's founding and once considered critical to its continuing success. For others, "telling truth to kings," or addressing truth to those in power, is emptied of meaning when "We the People" is misunderstood as "Kings-R-Us." For still others, purported cultural crises develop so slowly that, like a frog in a saucepan heated slowly, they will be boiled to death before they even realize there is a danger.

The American Hour?

The story of Las Casas will be interesting to people in many countries, but it is specially telling for Americans. I first encountered *Las Casas Before Charles V* twenty years ago at Oxford through Carsten Peter Thiede, a friend and scholar who is now the president of the Reinhold Schneider Association in Germany. What moved me profoundly then, and still does now, is Schneider's notion of "Spain's hour"—and therefore by extension "Germany's hour" too. For I have long believed that what Spain confronted in the sixteenth century and England in the eighteenth, America confronts now—challenges that go to the very heart of the American republic, which George Washington called "the Great Experiment." In other words, America's current crisis of cultural authority means that the present period is the American century's "American hour," a critical time of reckoning that is fateful for America's future.

My conviction of the momentousness of America's present crisis is not unique. It is shared by many contemporary observers. What will determine the outcome is whether Americans are sufficiently vigilant in understanding and addressing the crises that assail the republic today. The troubling suspicion is that in many circles, many Americans, including many American leaders, simply do not understand either the character of the American experiment as constructed by the founders or the character of its crisis today. In the person and voice of Reinhold Schneider's Bartolomé de Las Casas we might ponder the question of the condition of this extraordinary country at this extraordinary moment.

Telling Truth to Kings

REINHOLD SCHNEIDER

There was the usual confusion on the pier. Under the burning sun, young seamen rolled water barrels into the boats, while half-naked natives staggered along under their cruel burdens, driven forward by the whips of the overseers. Huge iron-bound chests were loaded on board under the watchful eyes of wild-looking and audacious soldiers. Travelers took leave of their relatives and friends. Here and there sickly and ragged Spaniards squatted on the stones, gazing longingly at the tossing barges rowed by natives or at the passengers climbing aboard the sailing ships.

Suddenly a crowd surrounding a tall Dominican moved towards the ships. Walking beside the monk, and carrying his baggage, was a man of lighter color than that usual among the Aztecs and of a build different from theirs, an Indian who might have been born in the Antilles. The two were the center of a colorful group of natives—men and shy, slim boys who looked up at the monk and pressed against his habit; and women, carrying children in their arms, who begged again and again for the priest's benediction. The monk stopped and the crowd immediately gave way, as if it were a sensitive and exotic plant closing up at the slightest danger of a touch. The priest saw that many around him had adorned themselves with feathers of rarest birds, such as are found only in remotest regions. A woman unfurled a feather coat of wondrous colors which shimmered and shone in the sun. She dared not speak, but merely tendered it and looked beseechingly at the priest with her dark eyes, which, like those of all her people, seemed to glisten with unshed tears. "Take it all, Comacho," said the monk in the native tongue of his servant, "and give me my bundle." While the jubilant natives piled their gifts in Comacho's arms, the monk bent over the children and laid his hand on their shining black hair.

One of the sailors whose duty it was to keep unauthorized persons away from the barges grumbled that Las Casas apparently wanted to take all his protégés with him even aboard ship. A richly clad Spanish planter who, to while away the time, had himself carried past the scene in a hammock by two natives, expressed in his clipped Spanish the wish that the Father, together with his ship, might plunge to the bottom of the sea. "It's worth a shipwreck to get this agitator out of the world at last!" His loudly spoken words were intended for Las Casas' ears. To taunt the Dominican even more, the speaker struck a heavy blow at the slave who ran beside the hammock with a parasol of palm-fronds to protect his master from the sun. "Even more useless by heaven, than these useless beings who can't even protect a Christian from the sun are those who would free these idlers," the Spaniard called back over his shoulder as his head bobbed away among those of the crowd. An angry flush suffused the Father's face, but at that moment the Indians gathered more closely around him, crying loudly. He blessed the women and embraced two men who seemed to be of noble descent, although clad in rags like the others.

"I will surely return," he said in a firm voice, "and I promise you that help will come. There is a just God in heaven. In Him you must believe. And on earth there is a just, God-fearing Emperor. To him I will go to ask protection for you against your tyrants." With this, he boarded the boat, speaking sharply to a sailor who tried to prevent Comacho from following him with his colorful burdens. While the faithful servant went below to busy himself in the hold of the ship, Las Casas remained on deck.

The milling and straining of the fear-crazed slaves became more frenzied as the moment of the vessels' departure drew near. At last the ships of the fleet began to slip out of the harbor. When the ship carrying Las Casas weighed anchor, the monk leaped onto a bale of goods. He raised his strong arm and made the sign of the cross over the forlorn flock, as if to place them under powerful protection. Those he had blessed sank to their knees and humbly crossed themselves. The Father was deeply touched when he saw that not only the baptized, in their threadbare woolen coats, reverently crossed themselves, but that the half-naked others did so too, even though he had been unable to baptize them for lack of time for proper instruction. He knew that, in the next instant, Spanish soldiers would swoop down on his friends and scatter them, or do even worse. In order not to provoke his countrymen to commit this final offense he turned quickly and went below. . . .

Heading out to the open sea, the convoy is scattered by a terrible storm. Las Casas helps not only the sick and terrified but the helmsman. He then comes down to take care of an aging knight who is returning wealthy but guilt-ridden after a degenerate career in the New World.

23

The Ballast of Decades

The monk's soutane appeared in the open hatch, above which the wind howled. Las Casas descended. As he passed the dim lamp, his face looked haggard. He walked towards the place where Comacho sat motionless. When his eye fell on the knight, he stopped, bent over the sick man, and looked at him for a long time. Then the priest observed in a low voice that he, Bernardino, must have been very ill. The cavalier answered that he found it ridiculous that he, who had made so many sea voyages, had succumbed to this one. It was high time that he returned home to live quietly on his possessions. Otherwise it might easily be too late to start the life in Spain to which he had looked forward for so long. But the recent tempest had really laid him low. He still felt as if he were dying. Las Casas lifted the little lantern which stood beside the nobleman's resting place and held it near his face and eyes. "Once there must have been a poison in your body; one of the strong poisons produced by the plants on the southern continent, in Darien and New Granada."

"That was long ago," the knight said curtly.

"Yes, but it is recurring. You have not recovered."

"We were among the first to explore the continent," said the sick man, "but it was then more difficult than it is today. The savages had fled. We found nothing to eat. We struggled along a mountain valley into which the Devil must have lured us. We did not want to turn back. We thought it had to end somewhere, but it did not. Then a comrade, unable to take another step, fell on his knees and crawled forward on all fours. This terrified us, but soon we were doing the same. So, like beasts, we came to a slope on which a few miserable herbs grew. We ate them without stopping to think. Only a few of us survived to learn how near we had been to a village and safety."

On the bared shoulder of the cavalier, near the neck, a red mark was visible.

"A scar?" asked Las Casas.

"Not my only one."

"But you must have received this one from above. How else could an arrow have struck you there?"

Bernardino wanted to answer evasively, but when he looked into the eyes of this priest who knew the souls of men, he kept silent.

"This is not the way," said the monk firmly but without harshness. "You must tell the truth if you want to get well again."

The monk waited for a while, but Bernardino turned his back, and would say no more. Finally the priest fell on his knees and prayed for some time beside the feverish man. The ship, seemingly helpless, rolled through the waves while the Father remained motionless with deeply bowed head.

From then on, Las Casas prayed more frequently and more fervently, often interrupting his work to lean his head on his hands over the papers spread out before him. He came to the side of the sick man but did not speak to him. One day, as he passed, the knight asked him how long he thought it would take to reach the Canaries. It might still take a good three weeks, the monk answered, for the ship was off her course. The other vessels were again out of sight, and nobody could know where God would lead them and how long He would keep them in danger. The knight complained that in such a period of enforced inactivity, no one could get well.

"A spate of inactivity is good," said Las Casas. "It is not during a time of activity that we mend. When it comes to action, we must already be well. I, for example, have not accomplished much in my life. Even the little I achieved, I could not have done had I not been forced to be inactive during my long voyages. Although we are always in God's hands, it is only at sea that we fully realize it. Day after day we hover between life and death, and we feel that there might not now be time enough to do the things we ought to have done. This becomes then our real burden and our cross."

The cavalier offered the Father a seat beside him, and then said: "I often ponder over my life. At such times I feel myself suddenly transported to the top of a mountain from where I can look down on all I have done and all I have seen. It is as if I could watch myself walking below, but along ways which have overnight become impossible for me to traverse again. Some of the things you said and wrote had reached me in those days, for even then I knew that you think that we have no right to enslave the Indians, that we have no right to their lands and goods, and that all Spaniards overseas live in a state of abominable sin and evil injustice. If that is so, then my life also, ever since I was twenty, has been one of utter injustice. But you do not understand us conquerors, Father Las Casas, you do not know what we are and how we were formed. You only love your Indians."

"I value the baptized more than the heathen. But my mission—the mission of every Spaniard in the Indies—is to baptize. That is our task and the only right we possess. It is for this alone that God has sent us forth."

"We knew very little about such matters, Father Las Casas, and cared less. There is much that I would like to tell you. The ballast of decades falls away from me and it is only now that I see clearly the road over which I have traveled."

"Only few things in life ever really come to an end, Sir Knight. Men and things may pass from our consciousness, but the mysterious burden which accumulates in our souls remains, and human force cannot free us of it."

"If only you could make it easier for me to speak," began Bernardino again with great effort, while Las Casas watched him quietly. "So many images whirl by me ceaselessly that I grow bemused. I feel as if I had lived in hell and had barely escaped at the very last.

"I crossed the sea with a Castilian nobleman who, with his younger brother, had outfitted two ships. Both men hoped to regain the fortunes they had spent at court and in the Italian wars. The caravels were sturdy, and the wind and sea were favorable. Never since have I felt so free and happy as in those long weeks when the wind drove us westward as easily as if it were child's play. At that time everything still seemed new. We met no vessel, and the maps we had showed little. We did not know for certain where we would land. But our hearts were not heavy even though we were conscious that every passing day left the familiar world farther behind, and that we would perhaps never return. Not all of us, indeed, felt this joy. Many had ventured out only to be able to return swiftly to Castile and lead the lives of rich men. When I had watched my servant carry my empty chests aboard ship, my ideas had not been so different from theirs. But as the homeland faded in the distance, so did these dreams which some of us had harbored. Now we were comrades. We all earned our daily bread the same way, and our fate depended on the same ship. . . .

"But that is not what I wanted to tell you. I wanted to speak of the pearls we then amassed. Never before had human eyes looked on so many and such beautiful pearls. I can still see the indescribable shimmering of the jewels as they lay piled on the rough-hewn table in the captain's cabin. We had acquired them more easily than a boy picks cherries. Our eyes glistened as we stood watching when the booty was being divided, each suspected the other of wanting to do him out of his share. We lived as if in delirium. I seemed to have lost all power of judgment. I did not even realize that the brothers, who stemmed from an even nobler house than mine, and whom I had always looked upon as men of honor, had suddenly become robbers and cheats. For a few dull mirrors and rusty scissors, which even maidservants would have scorned in Castile, they had obtained pearls rich enough to adorn the most venerated image of

27

the Madonna, and worthy enough to shine in the crown of our Catholic Queen. We had many more than we could ever have hoped for; we could have filled a sack to the brim with our pearls.

"But even that was not enough for us. We now had pearls, but no gold. And gold is more potent. It has greater power over the souls of men. It was as if something in us craved being in thrall to the shining metal. So we followed the coast of the continent westward past islands and bays. At the mouth of the Magdalen River a serious quarrel broke out between the brothers. We all took sides. Some wanted to sail up the river, others towards the Isthmus. Greed befogged our brains. Each sensed gold in a different direction.

"One morning we saw new land, but we sailed on, and by evening it had disappeared. We did not know whether it was inhabited, but later, in the darkness, we thought we saw boats following us. At daybreak canoes swarmed about our ships. The half-naked boatmen wore golden shields on their chests. They stared up at us, fascinated, then cheered and motioned us towards land. We followed them, anchored, and let down a rope ladder, but did not leave the ship. The native craft formed a wide circle around us, while our captain flourished the baubles we had brought from Seville for trade. He flashed mirrors in the eyes of the dark-skinned onlookers, and dangled chains of large glass beads in the sunlight.

"Finally an ornate boat, carrying the cacique and an oars-man, left the group and shot towards us. The chief climbed easily and skillfully up the ladder. Behind him came his servant, carrying corn-bread and a fowl, which, at his master's orders, he laid on the deck as a gift of welcome. The cacique was of a slim and noble physique, bearing himself with stately seriousness, and seeming entirely without guile. He returned the embrace of our captain with great dignity, but waved aside the gifts, indicating that he first wanted to look over the ship. With several others, I followed him and the captain below, as I was attracted by the demeanor of this native prince, and had already learned enough about the captain to fear the worst. Below deck stood one of the tall baskets which are used in Castile for harvesting grapes. When the captain came to it, he whistled, and two sailors ran in carrying ropes. While the two seamen secured the prince, our captain ordered us to guard the hatchway and to seize the Indian servant. The cacique looked silently at his attacker, the sadness of a nameless disappointment in his eyes.

"I have seen the disappointment of some men, when the fruits of their long and arduous labor melted away in an instant, and that of others, who had hoped to live in palaces and lie on silken cushions, when they realized they were to die under the open sky on a ragged coat. Disappointment is, perhaps, the lot of us Spaniards. But I have never again looked into a man's eyes and seen his spirit darken and, as it were, die. My heart was rent and at that moment I understood that this man too had a soul, one capable of suffering and destined for eternity. When I think back, I believe that this man's soul, in one instant, flashed forth and then grew dark forever. I wonder whether the Lord sends an angel to those who are falling into the depth without any fault of their own, an angel who will guide them to heaven even though they are not of the kingdom?"

The speaker, his cheeks burning with fever, looked at the monk. But Las Casas made no sound; his face remained immobile.

"Anger choked me," continued the cavalier, "when the captain tore the richly worked golden shield from the cacique's breast and threw it into the basket. He next thrust a wooden rod through the small neck of the wicker work, and thereupon leaned far forward, first touching the golden shield with his palm, and then sweeping his hand up to the rod. He repeated this motion several times, to make clear to the cacique that the basket must be filled with gold if he wanted to be freed. But the prince was so numbed from shock that he could make no response. His legs were tied, and his arms fastened around a post. He looked from the captain, to the basket, and then to his bound hands, the sight of which seemed to affect him most. I could stand this no longer. Releasing my grip on the servant, who would not have dared to move in any case, I stepped out before the captain. Though only half his age, I rudely demanded to know whether he was not ashamed to mistreat a guest in such a manner. With a laugh, he answered that he would rid me of my sense of shame once and for all. He ordered that I should be the one to stand guard over the basket.

"In the meantime the cacique had instructed his boatman to make the demand of the Spaniards known to his people. I was left alone with the prisoner in the dimly lit room. To free him was impossible because my comrades were on deck, watching for the golden birds they knew would soon fly into their nets.

"It was not long before the first Indians climbed on board. A few of them, probably the tribe's noblest and wealthiest, came below. Without showing their anguish, they paid their respects to the prince in what must have been their customary manner. They then placed their golden shields, their bracelets and their buckles in the basket, beside which I stood blushing with shame. The cacique thanked them with a gentle nod, and the men, after ceremoniously taking their leave, slipped away. We were alone again, and waited. The prince's wife came with their sons. In her arms she carried shining objects which she offered up like consecrated gifts on an altar. She was crying, but dared not touch the prisoner, whose rough bonds obviously caused him pain.

"Older men and officers then appeared who had but little to give. Some of them looked around the low-ceilinged cabin as if entranced. But as soon as their eyes fell on me and my weapons, they began to tremble. Others showed even greater respect towards me than to their prince, believing perhaps that anyone who could conquer their cacique must be a higher being than he. Old women came, carrying strange articles fashioned of gold— small lions and fabled beasts. In these the sight of their suffering master seemed to inspire the greatest awe. They looked long and reverently at his bound limbs.

"But at last the soft, shy steps on deck or descending the ladder were heard less frequently. The captain paced up and down impatiently. He kicked the basket and made the gold rattle; it was barely half full. The rod thrust through seemed to mock us. I saw that in our foolish dreams we had far overestimated the wealth of the tribe. The nobles appeared again, but this time with empty hands. They begged and wept for their master's release. And now I heard the sound of sobbing and wailing of the orphaned tribe coming to us over the waves and from the coast, accompanied by the music of strange instruments. All this served but to make the captain even more angry. In his blind rage he shook the basket. He drew his sword and placed its sharp point at the cacique's breast. The Indians rushed off with loud cries.

"The sound of weeping on the shore continued all night long. In the morning the muffled tones of the music moved farther inland. Some children came, adding small pieces of gold foil, but these new offerings were like drops of wine in an empty barrel. Tears of shame stood in my eyes. I felt degraded, and I sensed that this terrible humiliation would alter my whole life. I knew that I must either leave my companions immediately and return to Spain, or remain and become like them. For once a man has been degraded, he either succeeds in winning back his self-respect, or, failing, seeks to drown his shame in further debasement among companions sunk as low as he. I stayed on. I could no longer return. I knew that the gold fever which had driven me from home would seize me again as soon as I turned my back on the New Indies.

"Next morning the ship suddenly began to move. I saw that the sails were hoisted and that we were on our way to the open sea.

"Then the noble prisoner lost his long-guarded composure. He cried as I have only seen Indians cry—quietly but incessantly, as the rain falls into the sea. It is as if a limitless sadness and desolation would burst forth from them, as if their souls which have no knowledge of Redemption were trying to exhaust themselves into extinction. There must have been a mysterious bond between these people and their prince. For although those on shore could not have heard his weeping, his suffering must have cut deeply into their hearts. Such lamentation rose up after us that I, in my shameful place between the prisoner and the plunder, thought I could bear it no longer. But our departure was only a ruse of the captain. He wanted to squeeze the last ounces of gold from the natives. In all his coarseness and his cruelty he was a dreamer, as all of us Spaniards are dreamers. He clung to his belief that he had discovered the long sought land of gold and that the heathens were but hiding their countless treasures. He did not take his eyes off the coast as we sailed away.

"None of us had ever believed that a savage could be honest, but now, to our great shame, we were to learn how mistaken we had been.

"Screams and loud crying pierced our ears. The ship had been moving only slowly. It suddenly swung about and headed towards shore once more. I concluded that canoes must again be approaching us. I was right; but what the natives, now almost crazed with fear and anguish, threw into the basket this time, was poor, dull gold which they had probably feverishly dug up from the ruins of an abandoned settlement or from a river bed. With tears of despair running down their cheeks, they made us understand that they had given us all they possessed, and begged us to free their master now. Many of them turned to me and I, in this hour, cursed my voyage a hundredfold. I cursed the discovery of the New Indies and all the fables ever told in Spain about the New World.

"The captain must also have felt ashamed, but he hid it beneath his anger. He chased the sorrowing natives from the ship and then cut the bonds of the prisoner. The cacique, painfully stretching his tortured body, slowly climbed up the hatchway. We followed him. On deck, on the spot where the captain had embraced him on his arrival, he paused as if he felt that there should be some sort of farewell. The captain must have felt the same, for he handed his mistreated guest one of the cheap hoes we had brought along for trade. Some of us laughed. The cacique took the tool, looked at it silently, and then climbed down into the waiting boat, where his people received him with indescribable joy. We saw him ride away, sitting in the boat, holding the hoe like a scepter, his eyes fixed on the ship where he had been made to suffer such deep disappointment."

The speaker paused.

"And the gold?" asked Las Casas, seemingly unmoved.

"Soon we were to bring to mind the bird which had flown towards us from shore on our arrival. The wind and sea which had carried us to our goal rebelled as soon as we had reached it. The elder brother fell ill and died. No sooner was he buried than we saw how delighted the younger one, our captain, was with his heritage. Besides his brother's share of pearls and gold, he was now master of the entire fleet, to whose outfitting he, a spendthrift, had contributed but little. Now he boarded the other ship and set our course, still seeking the gold whose image glittered before all our eyes. Since the time I had stood guard at the grape basket and had not found the strength to change, I had become the most gold-hungry of them all. . . ."

The sorry tale of the knight's corruption goes from bad to worse. But it spurs Las Casas on the rest of the voyage as he works on the case he is to present on behalf of the Indians before Emperor Charles V in Valladolid.

The Council of the Indies

The Emperor's chair, only slightly raised, was placed opposite the long broad table at which the members of the Council of the Indies, the ecclesiastic and secular scholars, and the two opponents were now taking their places. The side of the table facing the simple throne remained empty. There were those among the assembly who could still remember the first entry of the young Monarch into Valladolid, and how magnificently the city was decorated when this Hapsburg heir to the United Kingdoms accepted his due honors in solemn ceremony. Now, by contrast, the servants had not disturbed the austere aspect of the rooms in which he was expected.

Cardinal Loaisa of Seville, president of the Council of the Indies, sat directly opposite the throne. The two opponents occupied the ends of the table: Sepulveda, his face inscrutable, bending over his papers; Las Casas, elbows on table, resting his forehead on his clasped hands, unmindful of the documents before him.

As the door opened, the assembly rose. Two imperial councilors who had been waiting for their Master midway between door and throne, bowed deeply; priests and scholars followed suit. Charles, a biretta on his head, entered, leaning on a cane. As the Sovereign approached the dais, one of the two pages walking behind him stepped quickly forward. Supporting himself on the boy's shoulder, the Emperor mounted the step and lowered himself slowly into the chair. With a curt nod he bid the assembly be seated.

Only then did he raise his eyes to survey the gathering with detached coolness. He noticed Las Casas, and greeted him with a soft, pensive smile. The monk responded by rising respectfully. Under Charles' unadorned black cloak glistened the golden chain of the Fleece. He drew the cloak closely about him and looked around questioningly. One of the pages hurried to the fireplace and awoke the half-dormant embers into flame. The Emperor was handed some papers, and these he began to study, holding his glasses at a distance from his eyes. A long time passed in silence, interrupted only by the Monarch occasionally reading a word in a low voice. Finally he looked up with tired, slightly reddened eyes, put his glasses away, returned the papers, and by a nod indicated that the Cardinal of Seville should begin.

"The presence of His Imperial Majesty," declared the Cardinal after rising slowly, "testifies better than any words to the high significance of this meeting. During the last few days it has almost seemed as if we were engaged in a literary controversy. Yet we all know that it is not to display his erudition that Dr. Sepulveda has written a book justifying the war against the Indians. This erudition," added the Cardinal with a slight bow towards the Emperor, "has long since brought him both the confidence of His Imperial Majesty and well-deserved fame. Dr. Sepulveda has written the book to reaffirm the rights of Spain to the New World and to demonstrate the justness of the Spanish government's actions. The Doctor's opponents must never forget that he has fought for what, during long years of study, he has come to recognize as the ideal most to be cherished.

"In this struggle," continued the Cardinal, "he has the advice and support of loyal men. He fights for his thesis for the sake of universal order and to serve his country.

"If, on the other hand, Father Las Casas has so far prevented the publication of this book, even despite its endorsement by high authorities and famous scholars, he has not done so, it is evident, out of envy of the Doctor's

35

name and reputation. Among all the reproaches which his well-known energy has earned Father Las Casas, lust for glory is never mentioned."

It was doubtful whether the mild irony of these words was intended to defend or accuse the Father, and expressions of subdued mockery lingered on the listeners' faces as the speaker continued.

"I consider it my duty," he said, "to help clarify the issue between the opponents, though to leave the decision to a greater insight. The two opponents," he went on, "personify two warring concepts, both of which are deeply rooted in the history of Spain and have long been basic influences in that history. Many of us have a Father Las Casas as well as a Dr. Sepulveda in our hearts. There can, of course, be only one truth and it will have to be found. As has been said, Las Casas prevents publication of the book not from professional envy, but from conviction that the Doctor's conclusions are false and anti-Christian; and he demands, accordingly, that, although free-born Indians should be converted, they should in no case be forced into the Faith. Convinced of this as he is, he must condemn the greater part of what has been done in the New World in the name of the Kings of Spain.

"If it is true that the cross is to conquer the earth by its own strength, without protection of the sword or of the state which wields the sword, Columbus should have left his weapons aboard ship before going ashore at Guanahani. We should have sent martyrs, not warriors, across the sea. In actual fact, more Spaniards have become martyrs in the New Indies than any chronicler has been able to report. Even Father Las Casas, who, as we know, has long been working diligently on a history of the New Indies, cannot account for them all. If it is wrong to use the sword, then unpardonable injustice is being done every day in the name of the Spanish crown. For even today Spaniards brandish their swords in the wild mountains of Peru and Chile, where the population refuses to be pacified. If we are not to think of the Father's demand as rash, or even insane, we must visualize clearly and in all their horror the crimes that he believes have been committed.

"A bolder request, of course, has never been made, as even the Father's friends have to admit. If this demand is to be met, the social order and way of life in the New World will have to be altered profoundly, though possibly only by degrees. The Indians will have to be given back the rights and privileges that were theirs before the discovery.

"What will then be left to the Spaniards is not our concern today. As for me, my only duty is to point out that the fight that Father Las Casas, after intense self-examination, has decided to wage can have the most far-reaching consequences. At this stage, the debate demands a decision whether, along with the way of life in the Indies, all relations between the motherland and the colonies should or should not be basically changed. For a change of spirit is the greatest change of all, and Father Las Casas' demand aims at such a spiritual change—one which would introduce an entirely new concept into the history of mankind. His purpose is to bring about the complete freedom of Man-before-God within the world-embracing Spanish Empire, whose structure he wants to see built in its entirety on the foundation of the Divine Law. However, it would be presumptuous to discuss before His Majesty the consequences which such a change would cause in the wealth of Spain, in the Imperial treasury and our Emperor's international policies. It would be presumptuous particularly now when His Imperial Majesty, after his heroic war against the infidels of Algiers, is about to unify the Faith and restore the old order so deeply shaken.

"Therefore, the ultimate question," continued the Cardinal in a lower voice, "is perhaps directed to the conscience of His Majesty; and it is whether Las Casas'

37

request or Sepulveda's doctrine comes nearer to God's command. The Emperor's conscience has to be the judge of how much secular power can be renounced or secular obligation waived by a divinely ordained Monarch who is desirous of fulfilling his duty to his Creator. That cannot be decided by any one of the priests and scholars here assembled, since they do not have the power to make their decisions effective. . . .

"I do not know how further to aid my cause if the force of its inherent truth is unable to do so," Father Las Casas began, having risen after a respectful interval. "For what I have here told you is the truth. Furthermore, we have not convened to discuss worldly affairs or the destinies of states. Wiser men than I are needed for such complex matters. What we must agree on is much more simple: how to follow the command of Our Lord Jesus Christ, who died for all men, and how to work for the extension of His kingdom without overestimating our own strength or underestimating the power of the Lord.

"The Lord has sent forth His apostles to baptize the peoples of the earth. The apostle's work will go on until He calls them to heaven. All of Spain has been entrusted with this high mission. The noble Queen Isabella was an instrument of the Lord when she heeded Columbus' plea and allowed him to prepare his ships—he, a simple and honest man, even though in many ways an ignorant one, and one to whom ill-intentioned opponents later did much bitter injustice. Our people must never falter in this holy mission. It was God's will that we discover the New World and bring the cross to those who He had long prepared to receive it. God will one day ask us whether we have carried out His will, and we shall be judged according to how well we have fulfilled this will.

"If I understand Dr. Sepulveda correctly, he believes, even as I do, that that is our mission. I, who wear the simple cloth of a priest, and often experience longing for the quiet of a monastery, now dare to step before the Council only because it is not empires we must win, but souls.

"We also agree, I believe, that God created Man free, and that there is, before Him, no difference between men. But the Doctor holds that we should conquer peoples in order to convert them, and only then, in a manner I cannot quite visualize, bring them Christian freedom after subjugation. But he who is baptized is taken into the fold and is freed of the burden of his sins. He cannot then be reproved for the error in which he lived before. Then he is a Christian under Christian law. He has been born again and he must adhere to the new life or fall under eternal punishment. Baptism creates a new man—that is the heart of the matter. If we chastise a baptized man for what he did before baptism, it is as if we forced an innocent man to atone for a crime which he did not commit. Our Lord transformed the world when He came and He transforms everyone to whom He comes. If we baptize men, we have no right to punish their former idolatry. If we do not baptize men, we have no right to be in the Indies. Therefore, I deem the wars against the Indians counter to Divine command, and the slavery unchristian!"

Las Casas had spoken under great tension and with constraint. At times it had been apparent that he held back angry words.

"I want to thank the Father for his moderation," Sepulveda answered, "and particularly for emphasizing what we have in common. Both of us have at times been in danger of forgetting this, as I admit and honestly regret.

"Las Casas speaks about himself," the Doctor continued, "and about his anxiety concerning the fulfillment of God's will. For the sake of the cause I shall also have to speak a few words about myself. Only with great reluctance did I accede to the Cardinal of Seville's demand that I present, corroborate and justify the reasons for the Spanish war in the New Indies. I have done so in the conviction of rendering a service to the Faith. For how can the Faith be advanced if not through an ordered state?

"At the same time, I have done so because of my great concern for the honor of the Emperor—who has favored me so often and has elevated me to be his historian. I have also been driven by anxiety for the honor of my people. The honor of Spain—I must say this, even though I would far rather clasp hands with Las Casas before the Emperor's throne—the honor of Spain has been offended. It has been offended by the contention that Spaniards under the noble and ancient flag of Castile, from the governor down to the humblest sailor—with the possible exception of the Dominican Friars—have committed nothing but the most despicable crimes.

"As for myself, I prefer the quiet of scholarly retreat to the clamor of public debate. If by conscientious work I should succeed in formulating principles which could serve a noble and wise Monarch in ruling his peoples, I would be perfectly satisfied, even more so if I myself could stay in the background. I am sure that all who know me will believe this assertion. For the sake of recognition by my Monarch I am ready to forego the applause of a gullible world. The Emperor's recognition has eased my life as a scholar, which by its very nature is a misunderstood and thankless one, valued and appreciated by few.

"Since I have acted for these reasons," he went on, "it has hurt me deeply when Father Las Casas, whose onerous life I have respected from afar, attacked my book with such bitterness and prevented it from becoming the good influence it could surely have been. It has hurt me that the Father, in his zeal confusing causes and personalities, has publicly degraded me, who am but a well-meaning fighter for the honor of Spain, and has even accused me of intellectual dishonesty. What has already happened cannot now be mended. Even the trace of a stain on a scholar's name is difficult to bear, but I shall forgive and forget, since I, at least, do not misconstrue the selfless devotion of the attacker, even though the attacker has not shown me the same fairness.

"Of course," added the Doctor, glancing briefly over the assemblage, "my basic conviction has not been shaken during the long disputation. The Father believes that it is paramount to recognize rights which are Man's by birth—rights which he acquires by being a human being. I believe, on the other hand, that rights do not exist by themselves, but must be derived from the organized state.

"The supreme law is to create order. Only after order is established can the demand for Christian life be considered, a demand which, to be sure, I recognize in its whole meaning, in its faith and in its hope. If, on the other hand, one considers the command of Christ as something absolute, and neglects its necessary relationship to secular order, it will, I believe, lead to a tragic confusion in human existence and, as the present quarrel almost serves to prove, can even lead to the endangering of a great and powerful nation. But the worst consequence of this unrelated devotion, which cannot possibly be the will of the Lord, will be precisely to preclude the fulfillment of Christ's commandments.

"For it will show that endangering a Christian state means the very endangering of Christendom, while strengthening the Christian state necessarily means the strengthening of Christendom itself. What serves to render this state strong is good, what weakens it, though not necessarily bad, is at least false and foolish. If a Christian state stands on firm foundations, so does Christendom in that state. The New Indies, from Mexico to Peru, from the Lucayos to the Isthmus, will be won to the laws of Christ only when they are subjugated to the scepter of the Kings of Spain. Measures which are designed to bring about this end serve the Faith. For this reason, I want once again to affirm my belief that the Spanish wars to subjugate and convert the Indians are fought in a just, even a holy, cause."

Las Casas had listened with growing excitement. Now he sprang up. "In the name of God, I declare that the Spanish wars of conquest are unlawful, tyrannical and hellish—far worse and far more cruel than all the crimes committed by Turks and Moors . . ."

"Nothing," Sepulveda burst forth sharply, "is more abominable than disorder—nobody more harmful than the agitator."

Deep abhorrence showed on the small face of the Doctor, but the eyes of the assembly turned towards the Emperor in fear that the untempered vehemence of the adversaries might arouse his anger. The Monarch still sat in the same, slightly relaxed, but not careless posture, the fingers of his right hand plucking convulsively at his left glove. Without a word he looked at Sepulveda, who responded with a bow and continued.

"It would be unseemly for me to defend Spain from such a reproach in the presence of our Imperial Sire, although there could be no better defense than to point out the well-known high-mindedness of our Monarch. But it would be against our dignity to prove that we are no Moors or Turks. It must bitterly sadden any well-meaning person that a wearer of the cloth, a man in the seventh decade of his eventful, restless life, allows himself, in his confused ardor, to be carried away and to insult honest men. Those men, trusting in the righteousness of their cause, could bear this wrong, were it not that he has also indicted his nation in the eyes of the whole world. For what could be more pleasing to the foes of Spain than to hear from Spanish lips that we have now been committing the most abominable crimes for years. And what if the world, which always looks for pretexts to take away from the privileged and the more fortunate, should deduce from these accusations that we had forfeited our rights, and thereby, our historical claims and our power?

"Father Las Casas' accusations do unthinkable damage to the name of Spain and, consequently, to the Spanish state. It is my duty to say this. It may even be asked whether a man who accuses his countrymen so persistently—by assertions proved unequivocally wrong by political philosophers—should not have to be considered a traitor. I will not mention the boundless exaggerations of which the Father is guilty in so many of his writings, and I will not go beyond the word 'exaggerations.' Also, I will not discuss the matter of the historical role of the accuser, which I have reflected on so many times. But it is certain, nevertheless, that the actions of Father Las Casas will seem the basest treason years hence. How much longer will it be before our foes take up and enlarge upon his accusations, unless an end is put to them, as I desire as a Christian and a Spaniard? We need fear neither the armies nor the ships of our enemies, but we do need to fear the destruction of our good name, which must bring in its train the destruction of our might."

Father Las Casas wanted to rise, but did not, as in this instant his adversary obviously dominated the situation. Sepulveda had the passionate attention of the assemblage, of whom only a few glanced pityingly at the accused. The implacable eyes of the doctor seemed to hold the monk in his seat. . . .

Dr. Sepulveda then switches to an ad hominem *argument attacking Las Casas for hypocrisy as one of the worst violators of Indian rights when a young man.*

Heavy on My Soul

"Such is the life of the man who feels himself called upon to pass judgment on his nation—on so many valiant men whose deeds outshine the utmost dared by Greek and Roman heroes. I do not charge him with evil intent. That he has offended some, that he disseminates obvious untruth, I ascribe to his fervent zeal. But the most ill-intentioned man is not as dangerous as the ardent follower of a false idea. We must judge our fellow men not by their intentions but by their effect on secular order and welfare. The judgment of their intentions and of their inmost hearts is not ours, but God's.

"I stand for the firmness of the secular structure, any weakening of which would swiftly make it impossible for our people to fulfill their tasks here and across the sea, or, indeed, to seek the salvation of their souls. As long as this structure is firm, we may aspire to the Kingdom of God. If the foundation is firm, present and future generations may continue building the house of God layer upon layer, in the hope that one day it will be completed. The firmer the foundation, the more promising our endeavor to draw nearer to God and to fulfill His law, or to perfect ourselves more and more in the spirit of this law. The state serves the Lord only if it stands firm. If the foundation quavers, we must strengthen it before we can serve.

"I fight Father Las Casas because he shakes the foundations on which our existence is based; because he brings destruction into our lives, and because he dares to act in this way even in an hour when the order of the world is given into the hands of our people, and when we must demonstrate to posterity that we are able to establish order, and to take upon ourselves the responsibility for the destiny of the world. Because we stand before this test, I bear witness against Father Las Casas. I do so, not for my sake, but as a servant of my Monarch, whom God has made organizer and administrator of the world. And I do so from deepest revulsion against the chimeras which befog the necessity for action and veil the clarity of secular law. We have already attained the most dangerous and glorious approach from which we can see and reach the loftiest pinnacle in the history of Spain, but if we now let ourselves be deluded by dreamers, by knights in white cloaks, we will fall headlong into the abyss. Our task is rooted in our might, and we would sacrifice both, as well as our lives, if we were to follow the 'Father of the Indians.'"

Sepulveda had delivered his speech, and particularly the last sentences, in cutting coldness, as if the accused were a well-known person who was not even present. The effect on the listeners had varied during the delivery. Open agreement had showed in the face of the Bishop of Burgos, an old adversary of Las Casas. He had endorsed some parts of the speech with a vigorous nod, others with a smile. Further, most of the scholars and councilors, particularly the Franciscans, seemed to have agreed with the Doctor; except for one of them, who had bowed his head as if in deep shame, and then covered his eyes as if to withdraw from what was going on. The chiseled features of the Cardinal had expressed displeasure. The Bishop of Segovia, who was sitting next to Las Casas, had had to force himself several times not to interrupt the speaker.

As for the Dominicans, they could not shake off a feeling of depression. Some of them threw anxious glances at the Emperor, who had shown no reaction since the early part of the speech when he had drawn his cloak even more closely around him, while others looked at their confrere with mingled reproach and pity. But as soon as Las Casas had seen through the plan of his adversary he had seemed to breathe more easily. Humility, resignation and relief had appeared on his face. Only when Sepulveda mentioned the trading in Negroes did the monk wince as if under a heavy blow. But he regained his composure during the final sentences and was now able to answer with humble calm.

"Dr. Sepulveda has studied my life with great care. What he has told is true, and I am grateful for that, because no weakness of those whom the Lord has made His servants should remain unrevealed. Are we not in truth just what God wants us to be? The Doctor was also correct in accusing me of inconsistency, of confusion and foolish deeds, or, in any case, of deeds which must appear foolish to the world. Yes, my life is burdened with guilt for which I can never do adequate penance. I have long since reached the age when others peacefully contemplate the results of their lives. I am now an old man, but in all the long years of my life I have not succeeded in living down my early mistakes. They remain, and wherever I go to fight for the Kingdom of God I meet the young Bartolomé de Las Casas who fought against this Kingdom and who is still strong enough to win against the aged man.

"Nothing lies heavier on my soul than the memory that I, as the Doctor said, advocated the shipping of Negroes to the New Indies to work in the place of Indians. On that one occasion I was not guided by right, from which we should not stray, but acted from pity. I believed that Negroes were hardier than the Indians whom I saw dying in every street, and I wanted to replace a greater suffering by a lesser one. But I was wrong, and thus became burdened with guilt.

"I herewith solemnly abjure my errors and declare that it is counter to every concept of justice and against the Faith— that it is utterly damnable—to capture Negroes like animals, to herd them into ships on the coast of New Guinea, to sell them in the Indies, and to treat them as they are still being treated day in and day out. I am guilty because I, a fool, gave in to my heart instead of advising according to what is right.

"It is also true that lust for gold dominated me in my youth. I am a Spaniard, and I succumbed to the temptations to which my people are subject. I have been fighting these temptations to the limit of my strength to show my people how they can be overcome. . . ."

Las Casas sorrowfully acknowledges his part but recounts his conversion to turn the tables on his accuser. His speech rises to a new level of intensity.

"Oh, that it were possible at all times to tell the truth to kings! If only the voices of men whose hearts burn with anxiety for the fate of their people had a different sound from all other voices! Or that those who know of hidden suffering should not have to keep silent! But there are so unbelievably few who live solely for the purpose of bearing witness, of reporting what is true and to what degree the lives of men depart from Eternal Truth. . . ."

Spain's Hour

The monk no longer paid attention to those sitting at the table. He stepped closer to the throne: "I am long weary of using arguments to support my fight," he continued passionately. "You can feed scholarship to a fool and he will grow no wiser. I have no more to say, and will never have more to say than this: *God does not allow evil that good may come of it.* We cannot attain good by evil means. And our means are evil.

"Oh, if I could but hold the mirror of truth before your eyes, my Lord and Emperor, it would reflect those evil means a thousandfold, and all who looked into it would have to blush with shame."

The Emperor had leaned forward and listened to these last words with growing interest and without a sign of disagreement. Now he made a gesture and said almost inaudibly, "Speak!"

This softly spoken word—perhaps only heard by the monk, although all understood the wish of the Emperor—struck Las Casas like a blow. He shrank back, and a terrible emotion gripped his body. Then he clutched at the edge of the table with his left hand, leaned on it, and drew a sharp breath. "I have asked permission to speak of what I have seen," he began, "and I shall try, although I do not know whether I will succeed. . . .

47

"All these things have I seen, and I could do nothing but make the sign of the cross over these mountains of corpses."

Las Casas staggered. He leaned harder on the table and the words now came only brokenly from his lips: "And that is not the worst. For I have heard blasphemies from those to whom I preached the gospel of love. I have helplessly watched the dying refuse the sacrament in order to escape the paradise of the Spaniards. Before my very eyes the souls of the doomed plunged down into eternal damnation.

"And what cries of anguish have I not heard! The cries of those who died under the lash, and of those who were burned alive, and of those stretched on the rack—and these cries were still not the worst. Worse were the lamentations and the sobbing and the tears—and much worse were the questioning eyes of those who could not comprehend and looked up to heaven and searched and knew not Him who dwells there. Oh, what have I not seen! You asked me for the truth. That is the truth, and yet still not the whole truth. I have seen things even worse; things no brain dares to conceive, no lips to speak—sights that would fill even Satan with abhorrence. Oh, what I have not seen!"

He sank down in front of the table, pressing his hands to his eyes and shaken by convulsive sobs. Two brothers of his Order raised him gently by the arms and led him to his place at the table. Nobody dared speak. A sound of weeping filled the room. The Emperor, deeply moved, looked at the shattered man. Then he leaned back, shadowing his face with his hands.

When Charles looked up again, his face was deathly pale, as if wasted away. He looked towards the Cardinal, who arose and said: "Nobody doubts the deep Christian compassion which moves Father Las Casas. If we were free to follow solely the dictates of our hearts, even as Father Las Casas would we console the miserable, prosecute the guilty, and put compassion above every other obligation. And we will surely not reproach his ardent priestly heart for calling those guilty who may be guiltless. We believe that he truly suffers, but we ask ourselves whether this constant suffering does not cause him to see every wretched person as an innocent victim of persecution, which is not necessarily so. Who would deny, after the touching scene we have just witnessed, that Las Casas has a heart for the Indians? Whether he also has a heart for the Spaniards we often doubt. Could it be, then, that he, as some of his opponents maintain, misunderstands his own nation, and that it is for this reason that he bears testimony against Spain? And could it further be, as his opponents also say, that he advocates the liberation of the Indians because he cannot see that their suffering is nothing but the consequence of their own crimes and obduracy? . . . ."

Las Casas resumes his case.

· . . . "The Cardinal mentioned the opinion of some that my heart goes out only to the Indians, not to the Spaniards. Perhaps, they think, with reason, for the former call me their father, and the latter their enemy. But I affirm before Our Lord that nothing grieves me more than the lot of my own people. I know that those others who suffer innocently on earth are assured of the compassion of the Lord; and even for those Indians who did not become true Christians, or who turned away again from the cross, because it was the sign of the Spaniards, even for them there is perhaps still hope that He, in His infinite kindness, will take them into His fold. But what about us? What of Spaniards?

"Upon us fall all the blasphemies uttered against our Lord in the agony of death. Upon us falls the grief of souls who are trapped in a sinful life and will surely fall into damnation." The monk turned directly toward the Emperor. "That the souls of your people perish, illustrious Emperor, is what forbids me to keep silent. Consider everything I have said as unsaid or unimportant, reject my reasons and proofs and witnesses—except this: that we always face eternity and that in this instant the Lord is looking upon us. I, though unworthy, am a priest. You, my Emperor, are not a priest, and perhaps you do not know this deepest grief for souls about to be lost. But you, like your ancestors, are charged with the stewardship of souls, and your powerful arm must protect them, for they are God's property. Your people shall live not only on earth, but in eternity, and for this eternal life you bear the responsibility within the power and limitations of your office."

Las Casas approached the throne: "Your people are sick, help them to recover. Clear away the wrong which suffocates them. Whatever the cost, do not hesitate, for this is what God desires of you. Perhaps this is the hour when God demands a great sacrifice from you. Offer it, Sire; do not ask how the world will respond, or whether your foes will turn it to their own advantage; put your trust in the Lord. We do not know His ways. We know only His law, and His law we must obey. What seems foolishness to men may be the deepest wisdom. You fear the consequences, Sire, if you should eradicate wrong and reestablish right? Do not fear, trust instead, and depend on prayer. We will not cease to pray. And if your people become well again, is this not reward enough for you?

"Free the Indians, reinstate their rulers, whose rights are as authentic as yours. Make your people see that the Indians are also created in the image of God and deserve respect. This must be your mission. It shall never be forgotten and shall bring everlasting glory to you and to Spain. Now is the time for you to carry it out, and thereby show that you are the servant of God alone, not of men or of your country, and that you are King because your spirit is nobler than that of other men. Ask no one but yourself. Ask your suffering and your sorrow and your grief. Ask your love and your conscience. The voices of men cannot answer you, but if you listen, Sire, you may hear the voice of the Author of history Who at this moment wishes to use you and your crown and your country as His instruments and Who desires to expand His Kingdom through you."

Moved by the words of the monk, Charles leaned forward as if inclined to yield. Just then Sepulveda rose behind the monk: "Sire, if ever the voice of necessity, which must be heeded by princes and peoples alike, has the right to warn you, it is now. He who disregards this voice is never forgiven. Heed not the dreamer, he would destroy your empire."

"How will you serve the Lord with your power shattered?" cried the Bishop of Burgos, who had listened to Las Casas' last words with barely controlled bitterness. "Of what use is a broken reed in God's hand? Do not forget that the New World, like the Old, must subject itself to you, and that you can reestablish order only if you remain firm. That is your mission."

Las Casas seemed not to hear the voices. He looked unflinchingly at the Emperor, the greatest expectation on his face. "It is Spain's hour," he said softly, and after a long pause he repeated these words in an undertone of suppressed tears, the precursors of a tremendous disappointment.

But the Emperor remained silent and suddenly the old passion arose in Las Casas, the passion with which he had answered Sepulveda in the moments of highest excitement. But like his final plea, his passion was directed to the Monarch alone.

"What then in the New Indies," he demanded, "belongs rightly to the Spanish crown? Nothing but a mandate. The Pope entrusted the lands beyond the sea to the kings of Castile that they might open the hearts of men to Christ and that they might infuse the old order of the Indies with the new spirit of Christian faith, but not to overthrow and exterminate this order. The peoples of the Indies owe allegiance to their kings and caciques; no mussel of the sea, no grain of gold, no fruit of the tree or of the field is ours, not one *real* belongs to us.

"Our Lord Jesus Christ wanted to enter the lands beyond the sea. He sanctified our ships with the mission of carrying Him across. We should have been the Lord's sailors and apostles. But of this chosen fleet we have made traders and privateers; and of the apostles we have made felons and robbers. Oh, how proud we could have been of this service if only we had understood it! We should not have taken, but given. That was God's mandate. And what was our response? We asked, 'How much do the ships cost?' 'How much must we spend for the erection of churches and chapels?' 'It takes money for this holy mission, and this money will have to come from the Indies.' This, alas, is how our wise doctors justify our pillage. But what better could you have done, Sire, than to spend Spain's treasure? And if Spain had grown poor in the fulfillment of its mandate, what prouder poverty? . . .

"But the guilt has already become part of our lives," he continued in a melancholy tone. "All warnings have been in vain. Spain has missed her hour. Those for whom God's mandate still lives go about as fools, laden with all the sorrows of the world. Oh, that God would take me from this world, so that I would not have to testify for him! Oh, that he would not have smitten me with deepest insight, and that I would not have to say what I must say now!"

Turning to face the whole assembly, he drew himself up to his full height and said in a penetrating voice: "It is certain that judgment will fall upon this land. For he who fails to fulfill the highest duty bears the heaviest guilt. Therefore God's anger will fall upon this land. He will shatter its power and lower its scepter, and take away its islands and possessions. And if those who rise from the ruins accuse the Lord, and ask why he has brought this misery upon the land, I shall rise from the tomb to testify to God's justice. I will answer the accusers. God called upon your fathers to perform a great mission and they closed their hearts and would not heed Him. Like unto the Saint, they should have carried the Lord across the sea on their shoulders, but they carried Satan instead. God does right if he destroys the might of this land. Terrible punishment follows terrible crime!"

Las Casas, immersed in the spirit of his words, had not yet finished speaking when the Emperor leaped to his feet, clenched his fists in utter rage and moved to leave the chamber.

Priests and scholars rose hastily to do him obeisance. The Cardinal was dismayed, the Bishop of Segovia deeply distressed, the Bishop of Burgos triumphant. Indignation, mingled with a certain satisfaction, appeared on the faces of most of the others as they moved towards the door which had remained open behind the Monarch. Only when Sepulveda, with an expression of angry condemnation, had passed Las Casas, did the Father seem to wake from his trance. He sighed and passed his hand across his forehead and looked about him. But at that moment even the Dominicans, who had remained standing near the door, looked back despairingly at him and departed.

The monk, gaining support from the table, dragged himself back to his seat. He seemed suddenly to have aged decades. Again, as before the disputation began, he leaned his forehead on his clasped hands and thus remained, first in silence, then murmuring prayers more and more fervently, as if he wanted to resume, with the concentration of his innermost power, the battle which seemed so obviously lost. . . .

To the amazement of all, including Las Casas, the Emperor decided for Las Casas and passed "New Laws" on behalf of Indian rights. He also appointed the reluctant Las Casas Bishop of Chiapa to carry out his royal orders.

The Difficult Task Remains

Las Casas hesitated. His eyes still expressed his deep distress. Then the Emperor gently leaned towards him. "The most difficult hours of your life await you, for it is you who must sail to the Indies to uphold the new laws—you can do so better as a bishop than as a monk. You will inspire fury wherever you appear. The predatory landowners and mine owners, and the pearl fishers who live from the misery and death of the Indians, will feel that it is you who are mainly responsible for these laws. Perhaps they will not even permit you to set foot in Santo Domingo; perhaps they will try to murder you in the streets. But it is my hope that they will shrink from murdering or torturing a bishop. Not my power, only the high spiritual office can protect you.

"I too must soon face my most difficult days. I do not, indeed, have to fear death and torture, but all else my opponents would not hesitate to inflict upon me. Above all, I fear for the fate of my newest hopes, and still more I fear,"—he lowered his head in meditation and then raised it as if to listen to distant voices—"the ebbing of my strength, the immense desire for peace. When you begged me to let you continue wearing the habit of your Order, I understood you very well, even though I would not be able to match your fervor if I were forced to plead to continue in my royal garments. It would be different if you were able to grant me permission to wear your humble habit." His next words were said as if with great effort. "There is strength in the thought . . . that others will continue to fight by our sides . . . as long as we ourselves persist."

Las Casas, deeply affected, bowed to kiss the hand of the Emperor, who smilingly murmured, "Bishop of Chiapa, poor Bishop of Chiapa!"

. . . The Emperor's eyes wandered from the monk to his son [the future Philip II], who stood respectfully before the Dominican. Then Charles picked up Thomas à Kempis' book and smilingly handed it to the Prince. "On the last day of the disputation, Father Las Casas enlightened me about the relative unimportance of my secular office. But the true teacher of both of us speaks in this book. Let us listen to his words once more. Read us the beginning of the forty-seventh chapter in the third book."

Prince Philip read: "Son, let not your spirit be broken by the toil you have undertaken for my sake; and be not cast down by any tribulation; but what ever happens, let my promise be your strength and consolation. I am able, beyond all measure, to reward you. You have not long to labor in this life, and you will not for ever be burdened by your sorrows. Hold out a little longer, and soon you will see the end of all such evils. The hour is coming when all toil and trouble will be no more. These things pass with time, and therefore, they are little and do not last."

"Those, indeed, are words which fit Father Las Casas and myself better than you," Charles said. "But the master reaches into every human heart. Before we start any task we should imagine its completion and our death as if these events had already occurred. That hurts us at first, but later becomes our consolation." With that he rose, squaring his thin shoulders. "I will not see you again before my departure," he said to the monk, who was bidding him adieu. Then, standing beside the fireplace, now cold, he nodded once more to the Prince and the monk as they left the room side by side. . . .

In the meantime the priests whom Las Casas had recruited gathered in the city. They witnessed the ceremonies at which a nephew of Cardinal Loaisa made the "Father of the Indians" a bishop at the church of the Dominicans at San Pablo. In deep emotion Las Casas received his bishop's crook. When the prelates and priests saw him in his new vestments, each must have felt how great was the burden that pressed on his shoulders.

He himself seemed to suffer more the nearer the day of departure drew. With gratitude in his heart he greeted in

55

San Lucar the many priests who were going with him on the voyage. Many of them glowed with youthful, holy joy, and eagerly anticipated boarding the *Salvador,* the ship which was destined to carry them across the ocean.

The many insults heaped on Las Casas in Seville—even after his ordination in San Pablo—the mockery and derision he sensed everywhere in the port, in the glances of the lay passengers and porters, weighed on his heart more than it ever had before. The fleet was still waiting for the arrival of the widow of the Viceroy, Doña Maria de Toledo, who was sailing to Hispaniola to secure the contested possessions and privileges of her sons, the grandchildren of the great Columbus. Days passed during which the impatience of the voyagers grew. The admiral of the fleet, the duke of Medina, lived in fear that the weather would change.

One evening Las Casas, accompanied by the young priest and Comacho, wandered down along the river bank in the fading light, past the crowded ships. Las Casas, who had long been engaged in a quiet inner struggle, could no longer keep back his fears. He had, he admitted, argued with sensible men, to whom the fate of the Indians and of Spain was as dear as it was to him. They could not believe in the feasibility of the new laws, and, he said, he still could remember Dr. Sepulveda, whom he had met, after the Emperor's departure, on a street in Valladolid. The Doctor had passed him with a disdainful smile, like a man who, through a bitter experience, had been strengthened in the belief in his cause.

During this conversation they had reached a neck of land which cut deeply into the shallow mouth of the stream. There stones which the waves had washed ashore were piled on top of one another, and had been crowned by a huge wooden cross, whose broad arms seemed destined to bless or admonish the departing and returning ships. Las Casas sat down on the stone pile. He turned his eyes towards the dark stream which rolled powerfully down to the sea, and whose distant further shore lost itself in morasses and swamps and the wild tangles of plants.

"On my last journey from Valladolid to Seville," he said slowly, "I dreamed one night that I had to travel this road again and again under the burden of my age and of all the things I have seen. Perhaps I shall return to San Gregorio one day, and perhaps the Lord will pile many, many more years on my shoulders, but He will not lighten my burden."

The light of the sinking sun glided over him. He rose and looked up at the cross, whose horizontal bar still caught the sun's rays, although the rest was already in shadow.

"That we pervade the world with the cross," he finally said softly, "is not so important as that we, while doing so, be pervaded by it."

He turned, and they walked silently back along the bank of the river, which, now entirely darkened, pushed its way, turbulent and swirling, towards the impatiently awaiting sea. The wind carried the roaring of the surf to their ears.

Next day the fleet departed. The ships weighed anchor and entrusted themselves to the current, which impetuously drew them on. The *Salvador* grounded at the entrance to the harbor, and had to be freed with great effort. Then the sailing ship moved hesitantly to the open sea. To the astonishment and even to the terror of onlookers, she listed so heavily that many believed they saw her keel. Finally winds filled the sails of the lonely ship bearing the Bishop of Chiapa. The vessel, at one moment riding high, the next dipping low, hurried after the departing fleet.

two

The Crisis of Truth

OS GUINNESS
AND RICHARD W. OHMAN

We probably all have our favorite memories of 1989 and the near-miraculous collapse of the Soviet Union—the Berlin Wall being joyously torn down, flowers thrusting jauntily out of the gun barrels of tanks, the toppling statuary of Marx, Lenin, and Stalin. The Soviet empire had been shaken earlier, in 1974, when Aleksandr Solzhenitsyn captivated the free world with this ringing line from his Nobel Prize acceptance speech: "One word of truth shall outweigh the world." Then in the late eighties Václav Havel caught the world's ear with his ideal of "living in truth" and his maxim, "Truth prevails for those who live in truth." Those who would resist the evil empire from the inside had two options: to be stronger than the Soviets—a forlorn hope—or to undermine the empire of lies with the moral force of truth. This they did.

Yet when the cheering died away, many Westerners never stopped to ask whether truth is sufficiently strong to make such a stand in the West. In fact, it doesn't appear to be. Today we are experiencing a severe crisis of truth on both theoretical and practical levels. Any traditional notion that truth is objective, absolute, and independent of the mind of the knower is said to be naive and obscurantist. Instead, truth is "relative" and "socially constructed," so "knowledge is power" and claims about truth must be dismantled to expose underlying agendas of class, race, gender, or generation.

The old story of three baseball umpires provides a simple summary of such radical relativism. "There's balls and there's strikes, and I call them the way they are," says the first umpire (speaking with a traditional and Christian view of truth). "No, no," says the second. "There's balls and there's strikes, and I call them the way I see them" (speaking with a moderately relativistic view of truth). "No, no, no," says the third (speaking with a postmodern and radically relativistic view of truth). "There's balls and there's strikes, and they ain't nothing until I call them."

The crisis of truth has intellectual dimensions that can be endlessly debated, but we should not overlook the practical consequences. Truth in America has died not only at the hands of scholars but at the hands of politicians, advertisers, and preachers. We are all well schooled in the art of bending, shaping, and "finessing" the truth. Consider some commonplace examples.

In 1995 one of the most prominent American conservative politicians published a novel. The publishers built their advertising campaign around quotations from two of the author's leading critics—words shamelessly torn out of context so that what was intended to parody was instead used to praise. Questioned about the brazen distortion of truth, the publisher was unrepentant: "The only thing I'm missing," he said, "is the publicity of a court action."

No matter that again and again the same politician makes hay of liberal distortions of conservatism. With post-modern notions of the "death of the author" and of "original intent," "truth" is whatever serves you, whatever you can make stick, and whatever you can make work for you. "Truth" is successful public relations. Joseph Goebbels himself could not have been clearer.

Or take another example. In his best-selling memoirs, one of America's most popular comedians tells an amusing story about his appearance on a television show. The only problem is that it didn't happen to him but to another comedian. As the first comedian admitted to the *New York Post*, he liked the story so much that he paid his friend one thousand dollars to publish the story as his own.

Such a strategy opens up endless possibilities, including a lucrative business in selling exciting life stories to unexciting public figures. And why not? We already have a long history of prominent Americans inventing and reinventing themselves to general acclaim. Take, for example, Sam Clemens's creation of Mark Twain. In America, Mark Twain said with firsthand experience, "The secret of success is sincerity. If you can fake that, you've got it made." Groucho Marx captured the same protean potential: "Those are my principles, and if you don't like them . . . well, I have others."

After all, if "God is dead" and "truth is subjective," any self is possible. Character is an achievement, but personality is performance. We are each a tireless impresario to our own ever shifting images with endless possibilities of makeovers. So American headlines are filled daily with preposterous reports of middle-aged adults or their press agents solemnly announcing their reinvented identities and redefined roles—as if any of us could self-transform at will.

The contrast of these everyday examples with the American founders is stunning. "We hold these truths to be self-evident," Thomas Jefferson and his fellow revolutionaries solemnly declared. But few things are less self-evident and more alienated to contemporary Americans than truth. Vaporized by critical theory, manipulated by advertising, softened by psychological jargon, mugged daily by the public statements of political leaders, clouded by euphemism, cliché, and hype, truth in America is anything but marching on.

"Truth is great and shall prevail," Jefferson wrote, quoting a traditional Irish saying. Today such a saying is "more a prayer than an axiom," one historian countered. Or as Mort Sahl quipped, "George Washington couldn't tell a lie, Nixon couldn't tell the truth, today we can't tell the difference." In the 1960s when the White House "credibility gap" first grew due to endless misinformation about Vietnam, a joke made the rounds of Washington: How do you know when the president is telling the truth? When he pulls his earlobe and scratches his chin, you know he is being straight with you. But when he begins to move his lips, you know he is lying.

The Sword of Truth

As our own culture of lies worsens, we would do well to tackle the thorny issues surrounding a tough view of truth by grappling with the twentieth century's apostle of truth, Aleksandr Solzhenitsyn. Many Westerners today, however, know Solzhenitsyn's writings better than his story. For those, David Aikman's essay (adapted from a chapter in his book *Great Souls*) is the best introduction to Solzhenitsyn short of a full biography.

Fortunately, Solzhenitsyn is too stern for us to cozy up to uncritically. And he is too passé a "celebrity" to mesmerize us dangerously. But that is why he is most relevant right now. Solzhenitsyn's monumental contribution to his own country is successful and in the main completed. But his witness to us in the West is more telling than ever.

From a casual overview, it may be difficult to see how Solzhenitsyn's background gave him the inner strength to battle the despotic Soviet regime. He was not unlike many other Russians of his day: His humble background, good education, commitment to the communist dream, and success as an army officer all suggest that he would have worked within the system for his own advancement. Even after his wrongful imprisonment he could have kept a low profile, let the unpleasantness pass, and endeavored to reconstruct a normal life. He could have said to himself that the lofty ideals of communist dogma entailed a price to pay to make society better.

But the Gulag changed everything. There he saw the lies head on and could not believe them. He was introduced to deep levels of truth by fellow prisoners, giving him a new standard for his life. And he developed the ability and passion to strip away the rhetoric and pursue the truth even though it undermined and smashed his previous ideological commitments.

A keen insight into Solzhenitsyn's perspective can be seen in his autobiographical *The Oak and the Calf*:

> There are many things which I cannot see even at close quarters, many things in which the Hand of the Highest will correct me. But this casts no cloud over my feelings. It makes me happier, more secure, to think that I do not have to plan and manage everything for myself, that I am only a sword made sharp to smite the unclean forces, an enchanted sword to cleave and disperse them.
>
> Grant, O Lord, that I may not break as I strike! Let me not fall from Thy hand!

Solzhenitsyn's image of being a sword in the "Hand of the Highest" reflects his premise that the source of truth and freedom was to be found outside himself. In other words, his thinking and actions are under God's direction. This undoubtedly has given him the insights, discernment, and determination to battle against impossible odds to expose falsehood and reveal the truth.

65

In an age dominated by the threat of nuclear annihilation, we in the West were quick to embrace Solzhenitsyn's opposition to Soviet totalitarian rule. Unfortunately, we paid greater attention to his political opposition to communism than to the moral proposition upon which it rested. Truth, after all, has been the dominant theme of his life, character, and accomplishments.

Today, we too may miss the battle for truth that is raging right under our noses. Almost daily we face pressures that would push us into accepting wrong as right and right as wrong. And daily we can witness those who have succumbed: the person in business who uses misleading advertising, the politician's statements or promises that everyone knows will not work, the lawyer who twists the facts to conform to predetermined outcomes, the educator who offers courses that teach opinion as fact, the parent who tells a child that a little lie is okay because it really won't hurt anyone.

All this playing with the truth deadens our senses so that it becomes difficult to see a "big lie," such as Solzhenitsyn faced in the Soviet regime. Barring the Gulag, what will it take for us to wake up to the crisis of truth in our own lives and society?

Truth Is Freedom

We may ask ourselves, does it really matter? Is the crisis of truth really all that bad? Isn't it rather an abstract problem, best left to philosophers? Those who are Jews and Christians have their own powerful reasons for defending the importance of truth—supremely the fact that truth is essential to the trustworthiness of God. But two simple reasons reveal why truth is vital to all human beings, and especially to citizens of free democracies.

One reason is negative: Truth is essential to resist manipulation. If truth is dead and knowledge is power, then we are all vulnerable internally to passions and externally to manipulation. "Where there is no law," John Locke wrote, "there is no freedom." Today, however, the problem is deeper. For while we have law, we have law only and no truth by which to guide and restrain it. Therefore, law itself becomes a tool of manipulation. Thus Walter Lippmann goes further than Locke to speak to the modern condition: "There can be no liberty for a community which lacks the means by which to detect lies."

A second reason is positive: Truth is essential as a basis for freedom and fulfillment. Most people today view freedom only negatively—freedom *from* authority and control. They forget the positive side of freedom—freedom *for* or freedom *to be*. But freedom is not the permission to do what we like; freedom is the power to do what we ought. Negative freedom is therefore never enough by itself, as it lacks content and purpose. Freedom requires truth and truth is freedom, for only when we know who we are and what we should be will we be able to do what we ought. As Pope John Paul II wrote, "There is no freedom without truth."

In America, truth is dissolving into "credibility," falsehood into what is "inoperative," and barefaced lies into "aggressive marketing." Fifty years ago Simone Weil warned her fellow citizens in France, "We live in an age so impregnated with lies that even the virtue of blood voluntarily sacrificed is insufficient to put us back on the path of truth." Albert Camus wrote similarly of the difficulty of fighting a lie in the name of a half-truth already shrunk to a quarter-truth. Or today news anchor Ted Koppel says, "We have become so obsessed with facts that we have lost all touch with truth."

Are there enough who still care? The pundits of postmodernism tell us that truth is dead and knowledge is power. We must assert the contrary. Knowledge is power, but truth is freedom. As Aleksandr Solzhenitsyn and his stand against tyranny show, the words of Jesus are neither a slogan nor a cliché but a necessity for free people: "You will know the truth, and the truth will set you free."

One Word of Truth: A Portrait of Aleksandr Solzhenitsyn

DAVID AIKMAN

As a journalist and writer I have met and interviewed many great souls, including Billy Graham, Mother Teresa, and Elie Wiesel. But the one with whom I have had the closest contact is Aleksandr Solzhenitsyn. I have been familiar with his writings since the astonishing appearance in 1962 of his novel *One Day in the Life of Ivan Denisovich*. I have come to know a little of his remarkable family. Long before I embarked upon writing this essay (for inclusion in my book *Great Souls*), I knew that Solzhenitsyn would eventually be recognized, even by those who disagreed with him, as one of the most formidable intellects and souls of the twentieth century.

As a student of Russian at Oxford in the early 1960s I struggled through the first few pages of *Ivan Denisovich* in the original language, stunned by the vigor of the language and frustrated by the rich, thieves' jargon of the camps that brings the tale so vividly to life. As a graduate student I learned of the fascinating continuities of Russian intellectual and philosophical life before and after the 1917 October Revolution that brought the Bolsheviks to power—many of which could be seen in the ideas of Aleksandr Solzhenitsyn.

But real serendipity struck when I happened to be the only fluent Russian speaker in *Time*'s Washington Bureau, other than the bureau chief, in the early spring of 1989. It was then that Solzhenitsyn's U.S. publisher, Farrar, Strauss, persuaded the reclusive writer to give his first major interview in years to an American news organization.

It soon became clear that this would be no normal journalistic adventure. Solzhenitsyn at the outset ruled out any discussion of the momentous changes in the Soviet Union that had been touched off by the reforms of Mikhail Gorbachev. Second, he wanted the topics raised to refer to literature. Third, the Solzhenitsyn family wanted to be sure that what was printed as interview text was in fact what he agreed he had said. In effect, he would have close to a veto over what was published.

I swallowed hard, and went to work preparing for this extraordinary opportunity. I didn't realize at the time that the encounter with Solzhenitsyn would be the first of three meetings over a six-year period, ranging in location from Cavendish, Vermont, to Khabarovsk in the Russian Far East, to Moscow itself more than a year after he had settled back into life in Russia.

If the cliché that familiarity breeds contempt often applies to acquaintanceships with the famous or powerful, in the case of Aleksandr Solzhenitsyn, the opposite has been true. I never became "familiar" with him, but I certainly came to know him more closely than most reporters. In doing so, my sense of awe about his character and his gifts grew, rather than diminished. Aleksandr Solzhenitsyn is not perfect, and he cannot readily be described as saintly. But in every other respect he comported with my own understanding of a truly great man, a person who had single-handedly, in many ways, changed the world in which we live.

My first interview was arranged with the precision and discretion of a secret encounter with, well, a Moscow dissident. It was in May 1989, and the lovely early spring of Vermont was spreading through the buds of birch and maple trees. At the general store of Cavendish, a hamlet of barely a thousand souls, a prominent sign on the wall sternly warned: "No restrooms, no bare feet, no directions to the Solzhenitsyns!"

With my assigned photographer, I was guided by Solzhenitsyn's secretary to the fifty-acre Solzhenitsyn compound set in the hills behind the town. Nothing indicated who might live behind the wire fencing and the thick cluster of trees; there were no mailboxes or nameplates and certainly no signs. Perhaps someday a Vermont state historical marker will finally reveal that the greatest Russian writer of the twentieth century, and perhaps one of the greatest writers of any language, lived for eighteen years in this rustic corner of New England.

When I met him face to face, the writer belied the almost forbidding figure I had unconsciously digested from dozens of articles about him. Aleksandr Isayevich, to give him the traditional Russian first name and patronymic, almost bounded out of the house to greet us, accompanied by his wife, Natalya. The patriarchal beard framed the bottom half of his face, but what was most striking were his piercing blue eyes. I had anticipated, perhaps from the knowledge of how strongly felt his convictions were, a certain sternness of expression. Instead, I found myself facing a broad, utterly charming smile and a sense of comforting informality. The skin on his face was fresh-looking, the almost red-tinged hair thinning and a little unruly. Just to the right of the middle of his forehead was a scar from a fall he had experienced during his youth. He was ready for the interview, eager to get started without further ado or small talk, but neither defensive nor suspicious in his manner. I took it to be a good omen. It was.

The interview that subsequently ran in *Time* was well received, perhaps helping to untangle some of the confusing impressions about Solzhenitsyn that had coalesced over the more than a decade he had already spent in exile from his motherland. Partly because of his reclusiveness while in the United States, his refusal to embrace the culture and values of his adoptive land of refuge, and his outspoken Harvard commencement address of 1978, some of the hostile impressions of Solzhenitsyn approached the absurd. He was referred to as a monarchist, or an anti-Semite, or an advocate of theocratic authoritarianism as an antidote to Communism. The interview gave him an opportunity to dispel some of those misconceptions.

No amount of interviews, however, will ever really do justice to Solzhenitsyn's achievement as a writer and a person. The majority of his literary work, in the form of the more than five thousand pages of the Russian version of his *Red Wheel* cycle of novels, has still not been translated into English. It will probably take another thirty years before the literary measure can be taken of this particular epic. Nevertheless, Solzhenitsyn's stature is clear. Through the passion of his preoccupation with the truth about the effects of Communism on Russia, through his brilliance as a novelist and a documenter of that truth, through his stubborn resistance to totalitarian dictatorship as a person, Solzhenitsyn was partly responsible for the demolition of any moral basis the Soviet Union might have had as a global superpower and justifiable system of government. "It is you and your writing that started it all," an angry Russian almost shouted at him during his long train journey across his homeland to Moscow in 1994. The "it" was the collapse of Communism and the end of global superpower status for both the Soviet Union and its successor state, Russia.

A Young Communist

Aleksandr Isayevich Solzhenitsyn was born a year after the Bolshevik Revolution, on December 11, 1918, in the town of Kislovodsk. His mother, Taissia, gave birth to Aleksandr in circumstances of both grief and local political chaos. She was only twenty-three years old, and her husband, Isaaki, had been killed six months before in a tragic hunting accident. At the time Isaaki, a former artillery officer who had served with the Tsar's armies against the Germans in World War I, was only twenty-seven himself. Back and forth over Kislovodsk the armies of the Reds and the Whites fought bitterly for two years, executing hostages and presumed opponents of their rule. Finally, by 1920, the Reds had triumphed over most of Russia, and Kislovodsk was firmly under Bolshevik control for the remainder of Communist rule in Russia.

Taissia lived with her late husband's brother Roman and his wife, Irina. The family still occupied what had been a comfortable home, but because of the pressures of famine they had to sell off their furniture merely to purchase food. Solzhenitsyn as an infant was comforted, he said later, by an icon—a devotional portrait of Jesus Christ commonly found in Russian Orthodox churches and homes—that looked down on him in his bedroom. He also recalled vividly an incident in 1921 when Soviet troops rudely barged into a Russian Orthodox church service. The toddler, insisting on seeing what the disturbance was about, was lifted high up to observe the scene. He never forgot the incident.

His mother, meanwhile, was running out of money, and moved to the busy port of Rostov-on-Don, where she became

73

a stenographer. Solzhenitsyn stayed for over two years with Taissia's elder sister Maria in Kislovodsk, moving each summer to the house of Irina, his other aunt, in a village just outside. When he was six, he rejoined his mother.

Because of her late husband's role as an officer in the Tsarist army, Taissia had difficulty finding work. She and her son were reduced to living in a shack at the end of a dead-end street close to the center of the town. With no plumbing, drinking and washing water had to be carried in by bucket from a pipe outside the house. In this run-down, impoverished home Solzhenitsyn was to live until he was eighteen.

Solzhenitsyn had learned early to fend for himself, the "man" of the two-person family, so to speak. He liked to be alone, to wander in the countryside, and above all to indulge himself in the rich library of Russian classics that Irina had somehow saved. At an early age he became familiar with the great nineteenth-century Russian writers: Gogol, Turgenev, Dostoyevsky, and Tolstoy.

Irina's influence on Solzhenitsyn was not only literary. She was a woman of deep Russian Orthodox Christian conviction, and she regularly attended the small local church. During his summer vacation Solzhenitsyn went with her, absorbing the rhythms and rituals of the ancient Russian faith and hearing how central Orthodoxy was to the history and identity of Russia itself. Family conversation at his aunt's home was open and invariably critical of the Bolshevik regime; inevitably, what he heard from his own family differed sharply from the revolutionary propaganda being peddled at school and in society at large. He was, Solzhenitsyn admits, "slow in coming to terms with the Soviet world."

But he was not slow in discovering his destiny as an artist. "From the age of nine I knew I was going to be a writer," he told me in 1989, "though I didn't know what I was going to write about." When ten, he was bowled over by Tolstoy's genius when he read *War and Peace*. From the earliest age, Solzhenitsyn never stopped writing, even when imprisonment demanded that he compose and memorize only in his head.

Two childhood incidents made indelible impressions upon him. The first occurred at the age of ten, when members of the Young Pioneers, the heavily Communism-orientated Soviet version of the Boy Scouts, ripped from his neck the cross he had worn since early childhood. The ridicule he received from Young Pioneers after this, and the intense peer-pressure to join their organization, eventually had their effect; Solzhenitsyn decided to join at the age of twelve.

But the other event was in some ways more symbolic for the remainder of Solzhenitsyn's life as a witness to the tyranny of Communism. His mother had become friends with a young, talented engineer, Vladimir Fedorovsky, and his wife, Zhenia. Solzhenitsyn himself had spent much time in the Fedorovsky household, enjoying what he could grasp of the stimulating adult conversation. Then, in March 1932, at the very height of the Stalinist purges of suspected "wreckers" and "saboteurs," Solzhenitsyn was about to enter the home when he witnessed a nightmarish scene. Fedorovsky was being arrested and taken away by Stalin's secret police. His arrest came to embody the theme of Solzhenitsyn's major work, *The Gulag Archipelago*.

Solzhenitsyn and his mother lived in conditions that today would be considered destitute. Shoes and clothes would have to last for two years or more before being replaced. There was never really enough food or warmth. Yet few of his school-friends were much better off in the 1930s, a time of Stalin's massive collectivization policies and the almost total absence of any consumer goods.

Despite his poverty, the shattering experience of the Fedorovsky arrest, and the huge political tensions of the mid-1930s, Solzhenitsyn seems to have both flourished in school and embraced with zeal the still-new Communist regime. By 1936 he had formed in his mind the basic outline of what was to become his life's literary achievement, *The Red Wheel* cycle that sums up the tragic cycle of revolution and tyranny that was to be Russia's experience throughout most of the twentieth century.

By attaining the highest high school scores possible in academic performance, he was easily accepted into Rostov University. Literature as such was not a university subject, and it would have been risky in the paranoid 1930s to try to embark on a literary career. Solzhenitsyn took a much safer option: physics and mathematics.

Besides, the bright and passionate young man had by now been completely won over by Marxist-Leninist thought and had transitioned from the Young Pioneers to the Konsomol, the Young Communist League, at the age of seventeen. While pursuing his formal studies, he read as much as he could of the Marxist-Leninist classics, increasingly convinced of their correctness. He and his closest friend, a high-school classmate called Vitaly Vitkevich, devoured the works of Lenin. Yet even then, the admiration for Lenin did not extend at all to admiration for Stalin. Privately—and later, with profound consequences for each of them—they despised Stalin, convinced that it was only Stalin's diversions from Leninist doctrine that had brought about the crueler and truly repressive aspects of Soviet life.

They were both entranced by the world of knowledge and scholarship, so they enrolled in Moscow's Institute for the Study of Philosophy, Literature, and History (MIFLI according to the abbreviation in Russian). Vitkevich decided to study philosophy, and Solzhenitsyn literature.

At university Solzhenitsyn pursued Marxism feverishly, editing the student newspaper and continuing to reap accolades. He had been awarded a Stalin scholarship for academic achievement, and this provided a stipend considerably higher than a normal student scholarship. His diligent Konsomol and editorial work would certainly have opened the door to full membership of the Communist Party and other honors. He was on his way, it seemed, to a brilliant academic or literary career within the bosom of Soviet society.

The Invasion of War

Events from far outside Solzhenitsyn's own universe, however, came crashing in. On June 22, 1941, the Nazi military juggernaut roared across the borders of Poland into the Soviet Union in Hitler's most ambitious, and ultimately most disastrous, military gamble of World War II. From henceforth, Solzhenitsyn's life was to be picked up and taken by providence on a tumble through unforeseen and often terrifying circumstances. The often nightmarish ride might well have killed off other men, and it would have cowed most into silence and fear. For Solzhenitsyn, it became the pathway to indomitable character, to national leadership in a crusade for truth about his nation's history in the twentieth century, and ultimately to worldwide acclaim as one of the greatest literary and moral figures of the era.

In the afternoon of June 22, the train to Moscow bearing Solzhenitsyn arrived in a city in near-panic by the total surprise of the German invasion. At MIFLI, the decision was quickly made to abandon all regular course-work. Many students simply went directly to their local draft stations to sign up. Solzhenitsyn also wanted to volunteer instantly, but he had left his draft card back in Rostov and was not accepted at the Moscow registration points. Infuriated, he quickly returned to Rostov, seeking to enroll there. This time, it was physical problems from childhood, a groin condition that had not been properly treated, that got in the way of his eager Soviet patriotism. Now he had to fall back on the only professional opening available to him, an assignment as a village teacher to a rural hamlet called Morozovsk.

Had the war gone differently, Solzhenitsyn might have remained in his rural backwater for months or years longer. But by mid-October, Moscow was almost within reach of the German vanguard. When in a desperate effort to turn the tide, the Soviet high command ordered the mass mobilization of every able-bodied male, Solzhenitsyn was drafted into a rear-area unit. He was made responsible for military transportation using horses, and was reduced to such basic chores as mucking out the manure in the stables.

After pestering his superiors, he succeeded in being assigned as the courier of an official packet to the nearest main military headquarters of Stalingrad on the Volga. There Solzhenitsyn successfully persuaded key officers that his university degree and his mathematics training made him ideal material for the Soviet artillery. By late 1942, he was embarking on a patriotic pathway in artillery, the very segment of the Russian army in which his own father had served during World War I.

During this time he wrote with enthusiasm to his university friend Vitaly Vitkevich, who had become an infantry officer in a different part of the front. Despite the titanic nature of the military struggle in which the Soviet Union was embarked, he and Vitkevich—fatefully, as it turned out—resumed their discussions of possible future political options for their country. At one point, they even drew up a political manifesto, "Resolution Number One," for an imaginary new political party. Solzhenitsyn was still an ardent Leninist and Marxist, but he knew enough about the incompetence and corruption of Communist Party life in the Soviet era to grasp the need for political changes. He despised Stalin and made disparaging comments about him.

By the end of 1944, the tide of German military success had run out. The Soviet forces were now pushing them back from Poland into Germany itself. Solzhenitsyn had

been promoted to captain and evidently enjoyed the privileges available to a Soviet officer, including epaulettes and
a shiny leather belt, side arms in a holster, and a star on the
cap. The military action was fast and intensely stimulating
for a man of his intellectual curiosity. In his correspondence
with Vitaly, he was eager to explore their common interest in political ideas and speculation. In one letter he had
referred to Stalin not by name—out of a perfunctory worry
that military censorship might disapprove—but by the
term, "the moustachioed one," a Russian word that also
meant, in general, something like "gang leader." It was a
terrible, terrible error.

By January 1945, the Soviet advance had taken Solzhenitsyn's unit into East Prussia and its handsome capital
Konigsberg. It was exciting for Solzhenitsyn to be on the
very ground over which his father had fought in Samsonov's
army in 1914, seeing first-hand the scenes of what he
undoubtedly hoped would be the locale of his future literary work. Rifling through an abandoned German farm
house, Solzhenitsyn came across a German book with small
photographs of famous Russian figures, including the late
Tsar and Stalin's arch-rival Leon Trotsky. He neatly cut the
pictures out of the book and kept them. Another error.

From Officer to Prisoner

The Soviet forces were massing troops, vehicles, and
equipment for their final push against Berlin. Solzhenitsyn's unit was busier than ever, so it was not an especial
surprise when he was told in early February to report to the
commanding officer, who liked and admired him, Brigadier-
General Zakhar Travkin. The general asked him to step
forward and hand over his revolver. Then two officers suddenly shouted, "You're under arrest!" Bewildered, Solzhenitsyn replied, "Me, what for?" The men didn't answer, but
instead ripped the officer's epaulettes from Solzhenitsyn's

shoulders and the star from his cap. They also took away his belt. It began to dawn on him that something political was happening. The two officers who acted so aggressively were not regular military officers at all, but belonged to the Soviet counter-espionage unit, *Smersh*, an acronym for the Russian words *Smert shpionam* (Death to Spies!).

Shocked and convinced that some terrible mistake had been made, Solzhenitsyn moved toward the door with his captors. Travkin, amazingly, told him to wait. "Have you a friend on the First Ukrainian Front?" he asked Solzhenitsyn carefully, in an act of almost insane bravery in front of *Smersh* agents. Angrily, the two men ordered him to be quiet. But the question had gotten through to Solzhenitsyn. Of course—Vitaly, his friend with whom he had corresponded. "I wish you happiness, Captain," Travkin said gravely, extending his hand for Solzhenitsyn to shake. And then the long nightmare began.

The two *Smersh* officers were so inexperienced with real combat situations that at first they drove off in the wrong direction, drawing salvoes of German artillery shells. They stopped and sheepishly asked Solzhenitsyn to help them find the way back to their headquarters. Solzhenitsyn obliged. It was not the last time he reluctantly found himself compelled to cooperate with the agents of Stalin's political tyranny.

Solzhenitsyn was convinced that before long everything would be resolved and he would be a free man. But he was desperately wrong. From the makeshift counter-espionage headquarters, he was marched to a railroad station in Poland from where he was taken into Belorussia. He found himself among a handful of "liberated" Russian prisoners of war who were immediately being moved from imprisonment in an enemy state to imprisonment in their own country.

The early stages of arrests of political prisoners in the Soviet Union had been designed to humiliate, shock, and finally subdue even the most recalcitrant prisoner. In the windowless recesses of the Lubyanka, Solzhenitsyn was ordered to strip naked for a thorough body search, for a shower, for a medical examination, even for an obligatory shaving of his entire body hair from the crown of his head to his private parts. Solzhenitsyn found one of the most distressing of all the regulations to be the one that required all prisoners to keep their arms outside their blankets when they slept at night. Since a 200-watt bulb burned in each cell day and night and wardens frequently glimpsed into the cells through peepholes in the door, the slightest infringement of the rule resulted in an instant and rude wake-up by a warden barging into the cell.

Interrogations were held, and in Solzhenitsyn's case no extreme measures were needed. Still a "Soviet man"—a believer in the fundamental cause of Communism and in the rightness of the Soviet system—Solzhenitsyn eagerly anticipated that once he could explain everything to the authorities, he would be off the hook.

It soon became clear that the only purpose of the interrogation was to provide as much tendentious evidence as possible to demonstrate the guilt of the accused and to force a confession. Dragged from his cell during the night hours, Solzhenitsyn was shocked to discover that his investigator, Captain I. I. Ezepov, had on his desk some of Solzhenitsyn's correspondence and the copy of "Resolution Number One." The rude comments about Stalin in Solzhenitsyn's letters, the discussion of the recent corruption of Leninism, the portentous demand for a new Leninist party: all were ample proof for the cynical Ezepov that Solzhenitsyn was guilty under Article 58, paragraph 10 of the Soviet criminal code: "propaganda or agitation containing an appeal to overthrow, undermine, or weaken the Soviet regime, or to commit individual counter-revolutionary acts. . . ." But what Ezepov wanted to add to Solzhenitsyn's charge-sheet was clause 11: "any type of organizational activity directed

81

towards the preparation of commission of crimes dealt with in the present chapter. . . ."

Solzhenitsyn was unable to protest, and was forced into a cell that eventually housed four other inmates, all of them caught up in the lunatic paranoia of Soviet judicial vin-dictiveness at the end of World War II. It was from these men that Solzhenitsyn first began to see close up, as it were through the microscope of upturned individual lives, just what Soviet power had wrought in his beloved Russia.

A Crumbling World

While the interrogations and the waiting for sentences wore on, World War II came to an end. On May 9, the Lubyanka inmates heard Moscow erupt in the biggest fire-works display ever as the citizenry celebrated the defeat of the Nazis. Not long afterward, his judicial stage of arrest now over, Solzhenitsyn was moved to another Moscow prison, the Butyrki, to await sentencing and transfer to what were to become a series of "islands" in the "archipel-ago" of prisons, labor camps, and transit stops that com-prised the entire "Gulag Archipelago."

The word *gulag* is yet another Russian acronym that in English translation means "Main Administration of the Camps." It was in the Butyrki that, sitting alone in a room with a bored MVD (Russian initials for Ministry of Inter-nal Affairs) officer, Solzhenitsyn found out that he had been handed down a sentence of eight years of corrective labor, a relatively mild sentence considering the almost routine award of "tenners" (ten years) for indescribably trivial offenses. The entire procedure was probably not unlike being given a piece of paper with a test-drive date at the Department of Motor Vehicles.

From Butyrki, Solzhenitsyn was moved to other Moscow prisons, where he experienced the way in which ordinary criminal prisoners preyed on the softer and often naive "politicals." He also learned more of the brutal ways of prison: the need to act with enormous cunning, to avoid "general duties" (the most arduous camp labor), and to be extremely wary of the hard-core inmate thugs and their gangs.

A move to a Moscow camp called Kaluga Gate brought him face to face with one of the most insidious pressures ever asserted against denizens of the Gulag: recruitment as an informer. To his regret for the rest of his life, Solzhenitsyn agreed under threat of serious consequences to inform a prison security official if he heard of plans to escape among fellow-prisoners. In fact, he never informed upon anyone, demonstrating the first hint of determined resistance to the gulag even as he became familiar with it.

All the while, Solzhenitsyn's philosophical world was slowly crumbling. In Butyrki he had engaged in long debates with two Moscow intellectuals who were committed Christians, and who made mince-meat of his Soviet text-book atheism. They shared his disdain for Stalin, but went far beyond it. To his astonishment, these young men also in their mid-twenties had contempt for the entire Soviet revolutionary experiment. It amazed him that people who had been educated within the Soviet matrix could reject the core principles and comforting promises of a bright new future that he had taken for granted. Meeting them also prepared him for the great sea change in his outlook, a shift that would not only ensure his survival but set within him the steel core of character and conviction that was to contribute to the collapse of the Soviet system.

If Solzhenitsyn had been dispatched to Siberian camps from the Moscow region in the 1940s, he might well have died. He was neither psychologically nor physically prepared for the appalling privations of the labor camp system. In particular, he was still a half-apologist for the Soviet system, well aware of its cruelties but not yet committed to an alternative worldview that could have protected his soul amidst the suffering of corrective labor. Providentially, he had raced through a recent book on the U.S. military nuclear testing, and in a fit of both *chutzpah* and cunning designated himself on a camp registration form as an "atomic physicist." He was nothing of the sort, of course, but at least he had some solid mathematical and scientific training from undergraduate days. What prompted the braggadocio were rumors that the regime had constructed special scientific institutes to take advantage of the often brilliant scientific minds among the political prisoners.

These unique scientific penal institutes were called "sharashkas," a name whose origins seem obscure. Prisoners transferred to them were permitted privileges unheard of in the gulag as a whole: proper mattresses, sheets and blankets, access to well-stocked libraries, exercise time, unlimited receipt of letters and books (subject to censorship, of course), and a meal regime positively luxurious in comparison with the watery soup of the prisons or camps. In July 1946, Solzhenitsyn was transferred out of Kaluga Gate to two temporary locations, including what became the most decisive prison experience of his entire eight years. This was the sharashka at Marfino, a former theological seminary in Moscow next to Ostankino Park.

The Freedom of Prison

The good treatment at the sharashka was evident enough in the food available to the prisoners. At lunch, for example, there was not only meat but actually dessert. Instead of the glaring, 200-watt light burning all night, the sleeping cell had merely a much dimmer, blue-painted bulb. Even more gratifying than the good treatment, however, was the companionship of truly outstandingly talented and moral fellow-prisoners. The nearly three years Solzhenitsyn spent at Marfino could hardly have been better designed to sharpen his mind, test his philosophical loyalties, and harden his emerging convictions.

In this respect, two men deserve particular attention. One was a brilliant, charming, and indefatigably generous Jew, Lev Kopelev, a literary historian who had been arrested on the same front as Solzhenitsyn. Kopelev's offense: he had been "soft on the Germans." Like Solzhenitsyn, Kopelev was a convinced Marxist-Leninist and believed his arrest was simply some horrible bureaucratic mistake. But the second man, Dimitri Panin, was almost his antithesis, at least on paper. A civil engineer who had witnessed the horrors of Bolshevik atrocities during the 1918–21 civil war in Russia, Panin was resolutely anti-Soviet and a devout Russian Orthodox Christian. He had first been sentenced in 1940.

Kopelev still believed in the rightness of the cause of the Communist Party, as long as Stalin was not in charge. So, at this point, did Solzhenitsyn. But Panin was implacably hostile to Stalin, to the Party, and to Leninism in any form. He was convinced that Communism in Russia had been literally a satanic importation from abroad, and that only God's supernatural intervention would free Russia from it. The three men would debate each other furiously, but as fast and devoted friends, conscious of each's intellectual brilliance and strength of character. All three were aware of how extraordinarily privileged they were. Not only were they serving their prison terms in remarkable comfort, they could debate the deepest philosophical and political questions without fear of being sent to prison. After all, they were already *in* prison. In fact, at this moment of Russian history, Solzhenitsyn's sharashka at Marfino was perhaps the freest location in the entire Soviet Union.

Solzhenitsyn found that he couldn't sustain in debate any support for Marxism as a system when confronted by the superiority of arguments against it offered by Panin and others. For a time, he didn't seem to believe in anything, having come to a midway point between ardent Leninism and whatever might have replaced it. He had resumed reading Dostoyevsky in the sharashka library and was influenced greatly. "I began to move ever so slowly," he told biographer Michael Scammell later, "towards a position that was in the first place idealist, as they call it, that is, of supporting the primacy of the spiritual over the material, and secondly patriotic and religious. In other words, I began to return slowly and gradually to all my former [i.e. childhood] views."

In this setting of relative safety, Solzhenitsyn cautiously resumed the project of writing a great historical novel about the October Revolution. His view of the original Bolshevik goals was still idealistic; he thought it was merely under Stalin that the excesses and the brutality had reached full flower. Of necessity, he could only compose in total confidentiality, inscribing his thoughts in tiny handwriting on sheets of paper that he hid carefully.

Panin was also becoming less and less comfortable with his own role as a coerced agent of Stalin's totalitarianism. When a tighter disciplinary regime was imposed in 1949, the added sense of repression caused something in Panin to revolt. He now refused to work on Sundays, going out to chop firewood instead, and revealing an almost brazen attitude of passive resistance.

Inevitably, Solzhenitsyn began to follow suit. He had already developed a habit of rapid-fire verbal delivery of complaints when the prisoners were permitted to address the authorities. Ostensibly, he was speaking only for himself, but his citation of official regulations on such minuscule matters as how much flour should be in the soup seemed increasingly like a labor-union representation of all the prisoners.

In effect, Solzhenitsyn was turning increasingly against the regime that had educated him, and in the validity of whose claims to power he had at least entered prison believing. He was influenced by Panin, who was rock-like and even quirky in his flat denial of the entire premise of Soviet life: the idea that a new universe could be constructed in any country by means of conscious social engineering. Solzhenitsyn was not yet entirely in Panin's camp, but he was skirting its outer borders. What undoubtedly pushed him finally into it was the reaction by the authorities to the two insolent miscreants in their midst.

On Rotting Prison Straw

On May 19, 1950, Solzhenitsyn and Panin were ordered without notice to report for transfer out of Marfino. They went from there to Butyrki for processing before being flung out of hell's "First Circle" into the outer reaches of Dante's inferno in the Soviet Union, the Gulag in its cruelest form.

In practice, this meant a several-week train journey in prison transportation wagons, fifteen men confined in a stifling compartment, through Siberia to a remote labor camp called Ekibastuz. Located in the middle of the arid Kazakh plain, Ekibastuz was dusty and stifling hot in the summer and buffeted by snow, ice, and winds of shocking force in the winter. The camp, with its double rows of barbed wire fencing, machine gun coverage, and use of floodlights, was emblematic of the Gulag as we have come to know it.

In Ekibastuz, more than anywhere, Solzhenitsyn learned first-hand the horrors of living in a "special prison." The daily, brutal labor, the marches to the worksites in rain, or slush, or cold so intense it was like a knife against the skin, the endless searches before leaving or reentering the camp, the waiting in line for the thin gruel, the absence of books, the brutality of the criminal prisoners—all of this day after day killed thousands of prisoners or turned the survivors into cowed or bitter zombie-like men and women. Determined not to repeat his early mistakes, Solzhenitsyn volunteered for nothing and avoided any possibility of being manipulated into a stool-pigeon.

87

The "special" category of prison at Ekibastuz required that all prisoners be known to the authorities in the camp not by their names, but by the humiliating procedure of numbers sewn onto their uniforms on their chests, caps, and trouser-legs. Solzhenitsyn's number was *Shch-262*, the *Shch* being the second-last letter in the Russian alphabet.

Solzhenitsyn found himself amid thugs, toadies, and weasels, but also with some utterly remarkable characters. One of them was Anatoly Silin, a talented Baptist poet who memorized vast pages of verse and who had pondered the question of suffering and its relation to the sovereignty of God. "Day in and day out he was meek and gentle with everyone, but reserved," Solzhenitsyn wrote later, and even recalled some of Silin's verse:

> Does God, who is Perfect Love, allow
> This imperfection in our lives?
> The soul must suffer first, to know
> The perfect bliss of paradise.

Silin's distillation of poetic beauty from suffering etched itself deeply in Solzhenitsyn's soul. Not even six years before his arrival in Ekibastuz in August 1950, Solzhenitsyn had been a cocky, even arrogant Soviet army captain, aspiring writer, and political reformer who paid scant attention even to his wife. He had believed firmly in the rightness of the Soviet experiment. He was a Communist. Now everything had been removed from him layer by layer: his belongings, his contacts with family and friends, his education, his very sense of self. Had he not experienced the earlier and comparatively easy years in the Marfino sharashka while he was maturing he might never have survived the Gulag at its worst.

In fact, he nearly didn't survive, for medical reasons. In January 1952 he was troubled by a large lump in his groin. It was diagnosed as cancerous and removed through a painful operation. As Solzhenitsyn was recovering he was visited by a Jewish physician, Dr. Boris Nikolayevich Kornfeld, who spent the evening hours fervently describing how he had just recently become a Christian believer. The following morning there was an uproar as Solzhenitsyn learned that Kornfeld's body was being carried out. He had been bludgeoned to death in his sleep by vicious blows. "On the whole, do you know," Kornfeld had said to Solzhenitsyn in his last conversation with anyone, "I have become convinced that there is no punishment that comes to us in this life on earth that is undeserved." Either Kornfeld had been an informer or the suspicion that he was had been stamped indelibly on his reputation.

The discovery of cancer, a murder almost weekly in the camp, the trauma of the operation, and finally the brutal death of a man who had spoken fervently and with kindness to Solzhenitsyn just hours earlier: all these coalesced in Solzhenitsyn's mind. There was no Damascus Road experience, no blinding revelation, but a slow, inexorable plumbing of life's greatest depths and the discovery there of a truth for which he had not been consciously searching. In some of the most powerful words of the entire *Gulag Archipelago*, Solzhenitsyn slowly, almost painfully, describes his spiritual awakening.

> Once upon a time you were sharply intolerant. You were constantly in a rush. And you were constantly short of time. And now you have time with interest. You are surfeited with it, with its months and its years, behind you and ahead of you—and a beneficial calming fluid pours through your blood vessels—patience. You are ascending. . . .
>
> Formerly you never forgave anyone. You judged people without mercy. And you praised people with equal lack of moderation. And now an understanding mildness has become the basis of your uncategorical judgments. You have come to realize your own weakness—and you can therefore understand the weakness of others. And be

astonished at another's strength. And wish to possess it yourself. . . .

In the intoxication of youthful successes I had felt myself to be infallible, and I was therefore cruel. In the surfeit of power I was a murderer, and an oppressor. In my most evil moments I was convinced that I was doing good, and I was well supplied with systematic arguments. And it was only when I lay there on rotting prison straw that I sensed within myself the first stirrings of good. Gradually it was disclosed to me that the line separating good and evil passes not through states, not between classes, nor between political parties either—but right through every human heart—and through all human hearts. This line shifts. Inside us, it oscillates with the years. And even within hearts overwhelmed by evil, one small bridgehead of good is retained. And even in the best of hearts, there remains . . . an unuprooted small corner of evil. Since then I have come to understand the truth of all the religions of the world: They struggle with the evil inside a human being (inside every human being). It is impossible to expel evil from the world in its entirety, but it is possible to constrict it within each person.

Solzhenitsyn's insights were the consequence of reality repeatedly smashing against the bastions of pride and self-reliance he had constructed. He was certainly not perfected by the suffering, and he retained plenty of personal failings and quirks that sometimes hurt others terribly and created difficulties for himself. But he was exposed in prison to the ultimate folly of a life based on the self and a philosophy based on a series of materialistic accidents. For a former ardent Marxist-Leninist, this was bitter moral medicine.

At Ekibastuz, Solzhenitsyn did not merely reflect passively on all of these insights but sought relentlessly to express them in his writing. The question was: how to write in an environment where it was a crime to commit anything to paper in permanent form except what the authorities felt they needed? The prisoners were permitted pencils and paper, but they were not allowed to keep anything written. Solzhenitsyn and others would therefore compose verse or prose in their heads. Solzhenitsyn composed and memorized literally thousands of lines, much of it later forming part of *The Way*, an unpublished autobiographical survey of his life that amounted to more than ten thousand lines, every one of which he had committed to memory.

A Divine Miracle

Solzhenitsyn's technical date for release was February 9, 1953, eight years after his original arrest. He was an infinitely tougher, wiser, more cunning, bolder, yet humbler man than the boisterous young officer whom the MVD officers had whisked from the Soviet army on the Prussian front. After release, it appeared Solzhenitsyn would be kept in permanent exile in a small settlement in Kazakhstan, miles from Moscow.

He took the only job he could find, teaching mathematics and physics in the local school. He lived at first in a mud hut with an earthen floor, no electricity, and ceilings so low he could not stand up properly. Later he was able to move to a slightly larger hut with a thatched roof. And here, night after night, he secretly wrote out the fruits of his memory. Terrified that he might be discovered, he composed on little pieces of paper that he meticulously hid before retiring for the night, initiating a habit that he maintained almost throughout his remaining two decades in the Soviet Union.

He loved the teaching job, but more importantly he relished the exhilaration of having no one barking at him morning, noon, and night. He was still under close surveillance by the local MVD and had to be exceptionally careful how he behaved in public. He was certainly lonely and was sometimes tempted to take up with local Russian women. But more important to him than physical or emotional needs was the sense of responsibility he felt to his manuscripts, to the men he had left behind in the camps whose experience with tyranny he would share to the grave. He made two fast friends, Nikolai and Elena Zubov, themselves political exiles who had also survived the camps. They became, Solzhenitsyn said later, "like father and mother to me."

Then, in December 1953, when he was just beginning to come into his own in this strange, almost monk-like existence as teacher by day and clandestine writer by night, catastrophe engulfed his health. He started to experience severe abdominal pains. A diagnosis confirmed it: cancer had returned. He was rapidly going downhill with the disease and under worst-case circumstances might have barely three weeks left to live. His only hope, they told him, would be radiation treatment in Tashkent. He had to get MVD permission to leave his place of exile for medical reasons, and could not plan the trip until the first day of 1954.

Frantic with worry about his still uncompleted work, Solzhenitsyn stayed up night after night despite the pain, copying out what he could on tiny pieces of paper, squeezing them into tiny metal cylinders, and pushing these into a champagne bottle that he buried in his yard of his mud hut. Only the Zubovs would know where he had buried his literary treasure. He never expected that a single line of his verse would be published in his lifetime. But he believed that, at some distant point after his death, men and women would read it with awe and fascination. Barely able to walk, Solzhenitsyn boarded a train and, as he recalled later, "set off for Tashkent to meet the New Year and to die."

But he didn't die. He was subjected at the Tashkent hospital to massive doses of radiation for several weeks. Slowly but decisively, his health began to return. By the spring of 1954, he was well enough to be released from the hospital. The radiation treatment had evidently killed off whatever remained of his cancerous growth. But for Solzhenitsyn, what had taken place was nothing less than the supernatural hand of God at work in his life. "With a hopelessly neglected and acutely malignant tumor," he wrote later, "this was a divine miracle; I could see no other explanation. Since then, all the life that has been given back to me has not been mine in the full sense: it is built around a purpose." On leaving the hospital, he happened upon a Tashkent church, went in, and gave a solemn prayer of thanks.

Telling the Truth

From 1954 until 1956, he worked away quietly as a teacher in Kazakhstan, austerely dividing his time into precise portions for schoolwork and preparation, and for his calling as a writer. But a great stirring in the Communist world had been unleashed in February of 1956 by Soviet leader Nikita Khrushchev's famous "Secret Speech," an astonishing denunciation of Stalin's crimes. By April, an amnesty was announced for millions of former political prisoners, including Solzhenitsyn. Suddenly all of the political charges against him were dropped. He was now a completely free man, permitted to live wherever he wanted in the country.

By December 1956, he returned to Ryazan and in the fall of 1957, he secured a regular job teaching physics and astronomy. But Solzhenitsyn's life followed no average pattern. The few major social contacts he permitted himself were with his old sharashka friends Lev Kopelev and Dimitry Panin. Once a year, in February, on the anniversary of his arrest, he would observe his own private "convict's day": twenty-three ounces of bread, water with two lumps of sugar in it, and reflection on his experience in Stalin's Gulag. But he wrote and wrote in complete secrecy, except for his wife and later a very small circle of trusted friends. Between 1957 and 1961, he succeeded in completing *First Circle,* his story of life in the sharashka, the first drafts of what became *The Gulag Archipelago*, and several plays.

It was the year 1959 that produced the work that was to change Solzhenitsyn's life forever, through him both the Soviet Union, and ultimately the world as a whole. It was a simple yet searing semi-autobiographical narrative of one man's day in the Ekibastuz labor camp, called *Shch-854*, the number sewn onto the prisoner's clothes. The only person to whom Solzhenitsyn showed the text, apart from his wife, was Veniamin Teush, a Jewish mathematician and political exile. Bestowing an almost Messianic blessing on the novel, Veniamin, according to Solzhenitsyn, "solemnly intoned Simeon's *Nunc Dimittis*: 'Lord, now lettest Thou thy servant depart in peace [Luke 2:29, KJV].'" Teush also added, according to another observer, "There are three atom bombs in the world: Kennedy has one, Khrushchev has another, and you have the third."

The story *Shch-854* might have slowly decomposed in the hidden archives of an obscure Ryazan physics teacher—Solzhenitsyn—had not the entire Soviet Union been shaken up by internal events in an unprecedented way. Khrushchev's famous "Secret Speech" in 1956, already alluded to, had released pent-up pressures for change that had been building ever since Stalin's death in 1953. Most important, it galvanized the Soviet cultural and intellectual elite out of their fearful passivity.

For several weeks in 1961, Solzhenitsyn had left a copy of *Shch-854* in Moscow in the hands of his old friend Lev Kopelev, who judged that the time might be right to submit it to a major literary journal. He and Solzhenitsyn agreed that the relatively liberal (by Soviet standards) monthly *Novy Mir* ("New World") might be the best avenue to pursue, since its editor, Aleksandr Trifonovich Tvardovsky, had made a moving speech at the Party Congress fervently supporting Khrushchev and appealing for writers to tell the healing truth about the horrors of the "cult of personality," as Stalin's era was euphemistically termed.

Tvardovsky, an expansive, hard-drinking, but generous-spirited man of peasant background, took the manuscript home to read over the weekend. In fact, he read it twice from beginning to end that night, not going to bed at all, and getting dressed at one point because he was overwhelmed by its truthfulness and power. The story totally engulfed him; he immediately announced that he had discovered a new, great writer. On December 11, 1961, Solzhenitsyn received a cable from Tvardovsky enthusiastically inviting him to Moscow to discuss the work. It was the writer's forty-third birthday.

It was also in a sense the birthday of a new existence for him. No longer the cautious, secretive, provincial school teacher, he was thrust quite unwittingly into the glare of a Soviet and eventually global publicity storm which did not let up for the next fifteen years. During that time, Solzhenitsyn's extraordinary character slowly revealed itself. His convictions never changed: He detested tyranny as much at the beginning of this period as at its conclusion, when he withdrew to Vermont. But his approach to the authorities changed. He began nervously, hesitantly, unsure of how far he could go in expressing himself. He ended up a roaring lion, a man who appeared to have lost all fear in his toe-to-toe challenge to a corrupt, dictatorial, and morally bankrupt political system.

Tvardovsky's ebullient approval of *Shch-854* was only the first stage of a tension-filled year between November 1961 and November 1962, when the novel finally appeared in *Novy Mir*. It first of all underwent a name change. Everyone at the periodical felt that *One Day in the Life of Ivan Denisovich* would be a far better title, and Solzhenitsyn acquiesced. There were other, tenser moments of confrontation between Solzhenitsyn and the editors at *Novy Mir* over various details, partly reflecting the varying degrees of Communist orthodoxy among the staffers.

The biggest issue for everyone, though, was whether the highest authorities of the Communist Party, including Khrushchev, would approve publication. For *Ivan Denisovich* was not merely a harrowing tale of a former political prisoner but a devastating revelation of just how brutal and arbitrary the entire Soviet labor camp system had been from the beginning. So tense was the issue that Khrushchev's own private secretary, Vladimir Lebedev, became personally involved, requesting certain minute editorial changes in the text to soften the blow of the story.

But still the drama was not over. In October, days before the issue of *Novy Mir* carrying *Ivan Denisovich* was to be printed, the Cuban Missile Crisis broke. The Soviet Union and the United States edged closer than ever before to the brink of a nuclear confrontation after Washington ordered missiles removed that the Soviet navy had brought into Cuba. The crisis miraculously eased, however, as the missiles were removed. *Ivan Denisovich* hit newsstands in mid-November 1962 from one end of the Soviet Union to the other.

The acclaim throughout the Soviet Union on publication of the story was instantaneous and unanimous. Since the work could never even have been published without approval by the Communist Party's leadership itself, the Soviet official press fell over itself to praise Solzhenitsyn. *Pravda*, the Communist Party newspaper, compared Solzhenitsyn to Tolstoy, though explained that the writer was merely advancing the Party's own cause of doing away with Stalin's personality cult. "The possibility of telling the truth has been affirmed by the Party and the people," it said. The government paper *Izvestiya* echoed this theme, with no less unintended irony proclaiming that Solzhenitsyn had "shown himself a true helper of the Party in a sacred and vital cause—the struggle against the personality cult and its consequences." Most Soviet readers, though, saw the story in a different light. For them it marked a new day of literary and historical truthfulness after years of official obfuscation.

Turning of the Tide

Solzhenitsyn's literary star was in full ascendancy. But it is quite striking, in fact, how quickly it began to fall in the Soviet literary firmament within a year of the glittering *Novy Mir* success. In 1963 he was nominated for the Lenin Prize, the ultimate confirmation of Soviet literary celebrity and official approval. But Khrushchev's effort to resume the process of de-Stalinization was itself under attack within the party. Few elements of that process were easier to criticize than the literary attacks on the "cult of personality" by writers who could be interpreted as harboring a more radical agenda. Solzhenitsyn was the most obvious target.

In 1964, the first major official rebuff came to Solzhenitsyn's official literary career when the Soviet establishment decided not to award him the Lenin Prize. Not long afterward, Khrushchev's secretary, Lebedev, refused the publication of *The First Circle*, which Solzhenitsyn had formally presented to *Novy Mir* and which Tvardovsky himself had warmly loved. Solzhenitsyn was in a dilemma. No doubt certain that the doors might never be fully open in Soviet society for what he wanted to write about, he had continued his meticulous early habits of copying his works and secreting them in hiding places around his home or among carefully selected friends. The most complete collection of everything he had written had been entrusted to Vladimir Teush.

With royalties from *Ivan Denisovich*, Solzhenitsyn bought a plot of land and a simple rural cabin in the village of Rozhdestvo, about a hundred miles east of Moscow. Working and living by himself, he was able to avoid the social and other pressures of Moscow, where in any case the political mood had toughened greatly in just a year. But although he was relatively secure writing in his hideaway, his very prominence and his views had now attracted the unwelcome attention of the authorities.

By a catastrophic coincidence in September of that year, an intensifying crack-down on Moscow literary dissidents and their suspected supporters led to a police raid on the Ryazan apartment of Vladimir Teush. There the KGB not only seized three of the only four copies of the novel *First Circle*, but all of Solzhenitsyn's earlier, and still unpublished works, including two stridently anti-Soviet plays.

The blow, hastily brought to him by a friend while he was at Rozhdestvo, was utterly devastating. Solzhenitsyn described it forthrightly as "the greatest misfortune in all my forty-seven years." He went on, "For some months I felt as though it were a real, unhealing physical wound—a javelin wound right through the breast, with the tip so firmly dislodged that it could not be pulled out." He even had, he said later, "thoughts of suicide."

Solzhenitsyn, in fact, had already attracted the unwelcome surveillance attention of the KGB simply through his friendship with Teush, whose anti-Soviet critical essays at the time were thought far more subversive than anything Solzhenitsyn had published. Listening in on Solzhenitsyn's conversations with Teush in the latter's apartment in Ryazan, the sleuths heard words from the writer's mouth that were astonishingly prescient and prophetic, coming as they did a full quarter-century before the collapse of the Communist regime. "I'm amazed that the liberal Russian people don't understand that we have to separate from the republics; they don't understand that we have to face this."

It was in 1965, indeed, that the highest organ of Soviet power, the Politburo of the Communist Party, focused specifically on Solzhenitsyn as an internal adversary of danger to the regime. While the KGB knew more about Solzhenitsyn's work and ideas than he realized, they still were flummoxed by his boldness and unexpected moves in what came to be a running cat-and-mouse game with the authorities.

For a while, Solzhenitsyn went into hiding after the Teush raid, convinced he was about to be arrested. But on realizing that this was not likely, he instead resumed his writing with intensity. He completed *Cancer Ward* in 1966, but *Novy Mir* decided not to publish it for the time being. Solzhenitsyn was becoming less of a literary star than a liability.

In November, Solzhenitsyn launched an open public attack on the KGB and the entire censorship apparatus of the country. In taking the offensive so dramatically, Solzhenitsyn knew he was crossing some sort of Rubicon in the relations of a Soviet writer with his government. "This was perhaps the first time, the very first time," he wrote, "that I felt myself, saw myself, making history." He was astonished by the explosive impact of his denunciations. "Almost every sally," he wrote, "scorched the air like gunpowder! How these people must have yearned for truth! Oh God, how badly they wanted to hear the truth!"

Solzhenitsyn seemed to be responding to a new sense of calling, not simply to write the truth in defiance of the wishes of the authorities, but to stand up against the authorities themselves. For two months during the winter of 1966–67 he disappeared from public view again, forcing himself into a drastic work schedule. Arising initially at 2:00 A.M., he would write for eight hours, rest for one, then resume for another eight hours from 11:00 A.M. until seven at night. His goal was to complete the second draft of the first six parts of *The Gulag Archipelago*.

Relations with Tvardovsky were meanwhile growing testier as it became obvious how antagonistic Solzhenitsyn was to everything Soviet. *First Circle* seemed permanently on ice. Then early in 1967, Tvardovsky made it clear that he would never publish the far less provocative *Cancer Ward* either, chiefly out of annoyance with Solzhenitsyn's radical views. That left Solzhenitsyn with essentially no choice but to publish his books in the West. He began operating an elaborate system with trusted couriers for moving all of his important writings for publication there.

It was in 1968 that Solzhenitsyn's life and career took on a direction from which there was no turning back. All of a sudden, his second two novels, *The First Circle* and *Cancer Ward*, were published overseas, causing an uproar in the Soviet literary establishment that echoed right up to the top of the Communist Party. He also began to take an interest in the activities of various dissidents who were challenging Soviet power. His speaking out on the Soviet invasion of Czechoslovakia in 1968 broadened his hostility toward Soviet rule from the well-defined issue of literary freedom to the much broader question of political freedom itself.

By the end of 1968, Solzhenitsyn was almost certainly one of the most popular figures in the Soviet Union. When he celebrated his fiftieth birthday in December that year, telegrams poured in from all over the Soviet Union. Other writers might have thought they had achieved what they wanted: national and international recognition, financial security from royalties, a position of seeming invulnerability in a totalitarian regime. But Solzhenitsyn only redoubled his efforts to tell the story that had enveloped his imagination since 1936, the epic drama of Russia in a decades-long struggle of revolution.

His sense of near-invulnerability, though, was the cause of a serious miscalculation. When the Soviet Writers' Union decided arbitrarily to expel him in November of 1969, he was taken completely by surprise and was unable to respond in his usual vigorous manner. He penned an intemperate response to the Writers' Union protesting the expulsion, which was formally announced November 12, 1969. "Dust off the clock face. You are behind the times," he thundered. "Throw open the sumptuous heavy curtains—you do not even suspect that the day is already dawning outside. . . . At this time of crisis you are incapable of offering our grievously sick society anything constructive and good, anything but your malevolent vigilance, you 'hold tight and don't let go!'"

But many erstwhile supporters of him for *Ivan Denisovich* did not sympathize with his venomous hostility to the society they lived in. For one thing, the Party authorities were bearing down on *Novy Mir* for having tolerated Solzhenitsyn so long, and many Soviet intellectuals preferred Tvardovsky's semi-acceptance of the Soviet dream to Solzhenitsyn's outright rejection of it. Solzhenitsyn wrote a separate letter to Tvardovsky after the uproar had subsided. "I feel that my whole life is a process of rising gradually from my knees," he said, "a gradual transition from enforced dumbness to free speech, so that my letter to the congress and this present letter have been moments of high delight, of spiritual emancipation."

Solzhenitsyn now found refuge at his most comfortable semi-exile to date, the dacha of the famous cellist and conductor Mstislav Rostropovich. The refuge was none too soon. The regime was losing patience with pestilential dissident critics like Solzhenitsyn. Had Solzhenitsyn been in a less prestigious location, he might have faced serious problems of harassment and worse. Increasing numbers of dissidents were being incarcerated in mental institutions.

Overseas, his novels *The First Circle* and *Cancer Ward* had stirred up such universal admiration that his name had cropped up as a candidate for the Nobel Prize for Literature. In July 1970 his name was formally proposed to the Swedish Academy, and on October 8 he received a call informing him that he had indeed won the prize.

It was reported that Solzhenitsyn was unwilling to apply for a travel permit to Stockholm for the ceremony out of fear that he would not be permitted back into his country. Later, it trickled out that the Swedes, unwilling to offend the Soviets, would not consent to a prize award ceremony in the Swedish Embassy in Moscow.

A Writer Expelled

What Solzhenitsyn could not have known was that his name was cropping up at regular intervals in discussions of the Politburo. What to do with him? At a meeting chaired by Leonid Brezhnev in March 1972, for example, several Politburo members spoke openly of expelling him from the Soviet Union altogether. He was, said one, "a degenerate," "a hostile person," "an anti-Soviet slanderer of the first order." Yet there was an enormous amount at stake too. Thanks to his enormous prestige in the rest of the world, there was no question of simply incarcerating him in an insane asylum, much less packing him off to the Gulag. The Soviet Union was in the delicate process of trying to establish trade, cultural, and arms-control agreements with the United States. It could no longer play the role of neighborhood thug in international affairs.

For the next two years, the Soviet authorities vacillated between spasms of bitter public vituperation against Solzhenitsyn and acts of spiteful vindictiveness. But it was in 1973 that the seal was finally set on Solzhenitsyn's fate in the Soviet Union. In September in Leningrad, the KGB arrested one of Solzhenitsyn's faithful copyists, Elizaveta Voronyanksaya, and interrogated her so brutally that she revealed the hiding place of one of the copies of *The Gulag Archipelago*. When the agents seized the manuscript, they knew they had one of the most damaging exposés of the reality of Soviet totalitarianism ever written. Solzhenitsyn, of course, had already secreted to Paris a microfilmed copy of the manuscript, but he had been unsure when to give permission for the YMCA Press to bring it out, so explosive was the material. Based on his personal experiences in the Gulag, on extensive research, and on material provided him by 227 other survivors, the full title of the book was *The Gulag Archipelago 1918–1956: An Experiment in Literary Investigation*. On learning of the manuscript seizures, and the tragic news that Voronyanskaya had committed suicide shortly afterwards, Solzhenitsyn gave instructions for immediate publication in Paris.

By December, the first volume was already in print in English in the United States and Great Britain, and the impact was startling. Even those familiar in some measure with the Stalinist terror could not fail to be moved by Solzhenitsyn's extraordinary detail. The precise methods of the arrests, the tortures used during interrogation, and the transportation system of prisoners around Moscow were all introduced with commentary. By turns sardonically funny, anguished, burning in slow fury, Solzhenitsyn accomplished something truly rare in all literature, the moral impaling of an entire political system.

The Soviet leadership was enraged. On January 7, 1974, a lengthy and urgent discussion of what to do with Solzhenitsyn took place in the Politburo. The mood was one of fury and exasperation. The *Gulag* was referred to as "a contemptuous anti-Soviet lampoon." When it came to what should be done with Solzhenitsyn, however, a consensus had now formed. First, the Soviet propaganda apparatus was to be unleashed against him full-blast. Second, as soon as Moscow could find a country willing to accept the writer, he was to be exiled there involuntarily.

It was given to *Pravda*, the official organ of the Party, to uncoil the vituperative whip against Solzhenitsyn. An authoritative article on January 14, entitled "The Path of a Traitor," rehearsed many of the early accusations against Solzhenitsyn—that he was a "counter-revolutionary," for example—but added to them a new gloss: he had been, supposedly, pathologically anti-Soviet from the very beginning of his career.

Solzhenitsyn was writing six days of the week, still measuring out his life in carefully calculated minutes, but on Mondays he would move into Moscow and stay overnight. Early in February, in the very eye of the storm raging over his head, he took time off to consider what the regime might do next. "Forecast for February," he wrote. "Apart from attempts to discredit me, they aren't likely to do anything, and there will probably be a breathing space."

He was utterly wrong. After weeks of searching, Moscow had found a country willing to take Solzhenitsyn. On February 2, West German Chancellor Willi Brandt had inserted into a speech the comment that Solzhenitsyn would be welcome, if he chose to come, to live and work freely in West Germany.

In the afternoon of February 12, the authorities made their move. Solzhenitsyn had come into Moscow the previous day, a Monday, and stayed in the apartment. He had already been summoned to the prosecutor's office to be confronted with criminal charges but had ignored the order. Now, two men from the office showed up at the door supposedly "to clear something up." Grumpily, Solzhenitsyn took the chain off the hook to let them in. Suddenly, there were not just two of them, but six, pouring into the apartment. "Nothing in my heart warned me," Solzhenitsyn recalled later. "I had lost my sense of alertness." Despite his intimate knowledge of how the KGB operated, he was totally unprepared for this sudden assault.

With the agents waiting impatiently, Solzhenitsyn returned to his study to find a school satchel to use as the repository of the necessities for prison, kissed his wife lovingly goodbye, made the sign of the cross over her, and with no further word was escorted to Lefortovo Prison.

To his surprise, Solzhenitsyn, despite his fame, received no special treatment in the very place he had first been interrogated almost exactly twenty-nine years earlier. He was stripped and searched, and taken to a cell where there were two other "normal" criminal prisoners undergoing investigation. The morning after arriving he was ordered to sit in front of the Soviet deputy prosecutor-general, who read an official decree. Solzhenitsyn was being deprived of Soviet citizenship and would forthwith be expelled from the Soviet Union itself.

A short time later, he was driven at high speed to Sheremetyevo International Airport, Moscow's principal gateway to the outside world. There, with no regular customs or immigration procedures, he was escorted to the plane. The flight had been delayed for three hours—officially for reasons of "fog"—while final arrangements were made to bundle Solzhenitsyn onto it. The writer had no clue where he was going, but he crossed himself and bowed to his homeland as he departed.

Arrival in the West

The plane landed and Solzhenitsyn saw where he had arrived: Frankfurt Airport in the heart of West Germany. He was welcomed by foreign ministry officials and driven to the home of the novelist Heinrich Böll. He was told by Böll to be as open as possible to the media swarming around and not to hide from the mass of photographers. But what could Solzhenitsyn now say? he asked himself. "All my life I had been tortured by the impossibility of speaking the truth aloud," he recalled later. "Now, at last, I was free, as I had never been before, no ax was poised above my head, and dozens of microphones belonging to the world's most important press agencies were held out toward my lips. Say something!"

Solzhenitsyn, paradoxically, felt that he had no new pearl of wisdom that he wished to lay before the world. There was, however, one farewell counsel from him to his fellow Soviet citizens that had been circulating, called "Live Not By Lies." He had been asked how one could resist Soviet tyranny without actively taking up arms against it. How could one improve the moral atmosphere of the entire country? In his essay, Solzhenitsyn responded: People should never permit falsehood to invade their conversation, professional work, meetings, or writings. It was a simple choice, he averred: "Either truth or falsehood: towards spiritual independence or towards spiritual servitude."

Solzhenitsyn had been assured that his wife, Natalya, and the children would be allowed to join him, and the Soviets this time were true to their word. In March 1974 the family arrived in Zurich, where Solzhenitsyn lived.

His exile had hardly removed him from the political and philosophical fray in which he had been a central figure since 1962. In March he approved the publication of his *Letter to Soviet Leaders*, a document that denounced the ideology of Marxism, warned of the dangers of any war the Soviets might conduct against China, proclaimed the Christian faith as "the only living spiritual force capable of undertaking the spiritual healing of Russia," and called for major political changes.

Solzhenitsyn continued to be highly visible and audible during his first few months in Switzerland. In December 1974 he traveled to Sweden for the formal presentation of his Nobel Prize that he had been denied in the Soviet Union. He was now able publicly to deliver his Nobel speech, a moving and deeply eloquent peroration that touched on politics, but only as a footnote to the very notion of artistic creation. "Art inflames even a frozen, darkened soul to a high spiritual experience," he wrote.

> Through art we are sometimes visited, dimly, briefly, by revelations such as cannot be produced by rational thinking. . . . And literature conveys irrefutable condensed experience in yet another invaluable direction; namely from generation to generation. Thus it becomes the living memory of the nation.

. . . In the struggle with falsehold art always did win and it always does win! Openly, irrefutably for everyone! Falsehood can hold out against much in this world, but not against art.

. . . Proverbs about truth are well-loved in Russian. They give steady and sometimes striking expression to the not inconsiderable harsh national experience: ONE WORD OF TRUTH SHALL OUTWEIGH THE WHOLE WORLD.

In Zurich, Solzhenitsyn gave a few interviews, one of the most interesting of which was in 1975 to the British journalist Malcolm Muggeridge. Solzhenitsyn told him: "In a strange way, I not only hope, I am inwardly convinced I shall go back [to Russia]. I live with that conviction. I mean my physical return, not just my books."

Home Again

In 1976, Solzhenitsyn and his family found a refuge from controversy and public debates in the village of Cavendish, Vermont. It was here that he decided to settle in order to complete *The Red Wheel*, his immense epic of twentieth-century Russia of which he had first dreamed four decades earlier at the age of eighteen.

Solzhenitsyn now set himself a punishing work schedule. Rising at 6:00 A.M., he would work in the morning, take a brief break for lunch, then resume work in the afternoon and only stop at night. He did this virtually every single day of his eighteen-year sojourn in the United States, seven days a week. (Presumably, there were some exceptions during religious holidays.) In the mornings, the family would gather for prayer to God to save Russia from Communism.

When preparing for my first interview with Solzhenitsyn in 1989 I had anticipated a somewhat crusty, distant personality. But I was taken aback by his physical energy and his warmth, charm, and patience with what at times were surely difficult questions. His eyes conveyed an intensity of purpose that I have seen in very few people in a lifetime.

Solzhenitsyn had insisted that no questions be asked about the turbulent developments then taking place in the Soviet Union, set in motion by Gorbachev. But in private conversation then and later he reiterated what he had told Muggeridge fourteen years earlier: He was certain he would return to his homeland a free man. His only precondition was that all of the judicial procedures that had been taken against him be annulled and that his books should be freely printed and distributed throughout the country.

Signs that Gorbachev was willing to meet Solzhenitsyn's conditions were apparent even in 1989. By September 1991, Soviet prosecutor Nikolai Trubin declared that all of the charges against Solzhenitsyn made in 1974 were in fact "baseless." By late that year too, Solzhenitsyn had finally completed the mammoth *Red Wheel*, a full five thousand pages. But in the Soviet Union itself events were moving at an unprecedentedly rapid pace. In December 1991, the hammer and sickle flag of the Soviet Union was pulled down over the Kremlin for the last time and in its place rose the white, blue, and red striped flag of the Russian Federation. Gorbachev was no longer in power and his place was taken by Boris Yeltsin, a former Communist who openly admired Solzhenitsyn. It was clearly time for the author to return to his homeland.

The great homegoing finally took place in May 1994, and in a manner none had anticipated. Instead of arriving to great fanfare at Moscow's Sheremetyevo Airport more than two decades after his forced departure from it, Solzhenitsyn, accompanied by his wife, his eldest son, Yermolai, and a BBC television crew, flew via Alaska to the city of Khabarovsk, on the Russian Pacific Coast. He had arranged to travel slowly back across the massive breadth of Russia by train, stopping frequently at different cities, meeting with local people and officials, and taking the pulse of the country first-hand after such a long period away.

What kind of Russia would he be encountering on his return, and how would he respond to it? In interviews just before leaving he said he thought his country's people were "sick to the point of total exhaustion." He eschewed any intention of becoming involved in politics. Whatever his emotional sympathies for the ethnic Russian character, he was uninterested in grandiose dreams of the restoration of Russian power. Indeed, in 1994 he reiterated a theme that he had echoed again and again through his writings: Nations, like individuals, have moral responsibilities to other nations. "We must build a *moral* Russia, or none at all—it would not then matter anyhow," he said.

After his arrival in Moscow and some initial major public appearances, including a speech delivered to the Russian parliament, Solzhenitsyn largely withdrew from public view. For several months he presided over a television talk show. But though his selected topics were always interesting, Russian society, impatient with seriousness and anxious to catch up with the rest of the world's notions of consumer enter-tainment, seemed no longer interested in serious discussions.

When I interviewed him once more in Moscow, in October 1995, Solzhenitsyn was as strict with the allotted time as ever and a trifle less patient with the media than he had been during our hours-long interview six years earlier. But he was still enthralling on topics that arrest the attention of serious thinkers about politics, society, and culture. He spoke of his country's "fatigue of culture, its emaciation," the decline of literature both in mass consumer societies and in dictatorships. He spoke warmly of patriotism ("a whole and deliberate feeling of love towards your country, your nation"), and yet of the huge need of repentance in his own country for the horrible wrongs committed there under the rule of Communism. He also took up the theme

109

of freedom and truth he had dealt with in his Nobel prize speech two decades earlier. He said,

> In the Gospel it says, "You shall know the truth and the truth shall make you free." It is fascinating, astounding. What does this mean: It means that the path to freedom lies not in the fact that the parliament made a law of greater freedom today, but [rather] that you have to go through the truth. And if you go through truth just a little, then you will no longer say things such as, "Well, if the people are good, truth doesn't matter."

I wondered aloud to Solzhenitsyn if he believed in the notion of calling, the idea common in the Jewish and Christian faiths that God summons people to accomplish—or at least to perform—certain things in their lives. His reply was swift. "Everybody has a purpose and the main purpose of each of us is how to understand it," he replied. "Given the everyday preoccupations of ordinary life, people don't spend enough time thinking about this. They have their daily troubles. Only self-deepening, reflection, prayer, only reflection can discover that purpose." Did Solzhenitsyn believe he had completed his own life's task? I asked. "At the end of my life, I will have fulfilled my debt," he said.

Debt? What debt? And then I remembered: Solzhenitsyn had spoken of his debt to those who had given him their knowledge of the truth of Russia under Communist rule, men and women who had died with no certainty that what they had told him would reach the light of day, much less help change their country. I remembered, too, a question I had asked Solzhenitsyn in 1989, whether his life in the camps was not something that he cherished—as part of his calling, so to speak—rather than regretted. "Yes," he said then, "because in those circumstances human nature becomes very much more visible. I was very lucky to have been in the camps—and especially to have survived."

three

This Too Shall Pass Away

OS GUINNESS

F orgive me for interrupting, but would you like to know
from the inside what it was like to succumb to Nazism?"
It was the mid-1960s and I had just finished lunch with a
dozen or more skiing friends high above an Alpine ski
resort in French-speaking Switzerland. Racing from topic
to topic with typical twenty-something intensity, we had
finished with a passionate discussion of Lyndon Johnson's
escalation of the Vietnam War and how "good Germans"
had been engulfed by the slow-rising tide of Hitler's evil
in the 1930s.

113

Perhaps it was because two of us lingered at the table behind the others. Perhaps it was because the older man's tone had something of the insistence of Coleridge's ancient mariner tugging on the arm of the wedding guest. Whatever the reason, it was four hours and several glasses of vin chaud later when we set off to ski down the mountain as the sun set in a fireball of splendor on the Dents du Midi.

The old Prussian's story was a mixture of pride, sorrow, and shame, unembroidered with sentiment or self-pity. But at its heart was a tale of compromise through a thousand silences—silences through which he felt he had become as much an accomplice of evil as if he had been a henchman of Hitler himself. Again and again he simply knew, he knew beyond a shadow of inner doubt that the claims were lies and the acts were evil. But he never spoke out and he never acted until his conscience was bribed beyond recovery and his compliance complete.

With deep feeling he quoted the well-known confession of Martin Niemöller, the pastor who initially had sent a telegram congratulating Hitler but also had been one of the first to wake to the developing horror: "In Germany they came first for the communists, and I didn't speak up because I wasn't a communist. Then they came for the Jews, and I didn't speak up because I wasn't a Jew. Then they came for the trade unionists, and I didn't speak up because I wasn't a trade unionist. Then they came for the Catholics, and I didn't speak up because I was a Protestant. Then they came for me, and by that time no one was left to speak up."

My memory of that conversation of thirty years ago was triggered by the events in the White House in early 1998 and the heated discussion around countless microphones and dining room tables of the public reaction to the events. Would the battle be won by power plays or the truth? Were the many broader considerations legitimate enough to excuse the troubling indifference of ordinary Americans? Or was this a defining moment in the evolution of American public morals, trumpeted by some as progress toward "moral sophistication" and lamented by others as "moral decline"?

Regardless of the eventual outcome, one could raise important questions about the misreading of the public opinion surveys in much of the commentary. One could raise deeper questions about the obsession with opinion polling—in itself a clear indication of moral change, as if questions of right and wrong, truth and falsehood, goodness and villainy, allegation and proof are settled by pollsters rather than principle. But there is no skirting the need to assess public attitudes that are fundamental to democratic life. And, in the case of the United States, the baseline from which we can judge was established relatively recently—a little more than two hundred years ago—and the earliest voices—the framers—were remarkably coherent and articulate about their concerns in this area.

Needless to say, not even today's direst interpretations argue that we are sliding into the infamous "night and fog" that engulfed Germany in the 1930s. And the issues at stake are far wider than any single incident, person, elected position, or country. But with representative democracy and market capitalism both riding high in the world, an urgent question persists for all the nations of Western democracy: Is the cultural order of our societies—the world of families, churches and synagogues, schools, colleges, the media and entertainment—doing a good job of cultivating free, responsible citizens? Or are we seeing not only corruption at vital points but widespread compliance with that corruption that makes us all accomplices to our own decline? When a nation winks at the wrongdoings of its leaders, it opens itself to an erosion that is hard to stop.

Kay Haugaard, whose essay follows, is a professor in Southern California and therefore refreshingly remote from the passions of Washington's "beltway fever" and the "feeding frenzies" of the national press and media. But this dis-

115

tance makes her testimony all the more telling. The essay was first published in *The Chronicle of Higher Education* in June 1997 under the title "Suspending Moral Judgment." This fascinating account of her years of teaching creative writing, including Shirley Jackson's short story "The Lottery," struck a chord in many readers, sparking widespread discussion. For as she tells so well, all the changing trends of the past generation were both reflected and brought into sharp focus in her classes' responses to "The Lottery."

Shirley Jackson's short story "The Lottery" was first published in *The New Yorker* in 1948. Since then it has been read and discussed in countless high school classes and the shifting responses to it tell us more about the state of the union than endless public opinion surveys and presidential speeches. Fifty years ago the stunning denouement of the story raised a storm of shocked outrage. *The New Yorker* was deluged with sackfuls of mail in response. In the 1990s, by contrast, moral judgments have become toothless and unfashionable. In a day of relativism, tolerance, cynicism, radical multiculturalism, and "morally ungrounded morality," how is anyone to judge anything, let alone condemn?

As Haugaard notes with dismay, "No one in the whole class of twenty ostensibly intelligent individuals would go out on a limb and take a stand against human sacrifice." The unthinkable has become all too thinkable. The 1960s student slogan "It is forbidden to forbid" now covers thinking and criticizing as well as acting. Censuring is commonly confused with censoring and moral judgment is paralyzed at the same time that gossip is unleashed. In many discussions even the Holocaust is increasingly "personally deplored" but left morally uncondemned.

Bertold Brecht's eleventh commandment, "Be good to yourself," has been replaced by a new candidate, "Thou shall not judge." What happens then is simple. When nothing can be judged except judgment itself, the barriers between unthinkable, acceptable, and doable collapse entirely. And then, since life goes on and the sky does not fall, the conclusion is drawn that the original concern was unfounded.

Nothing, of course, is further from the truth. But the erosion proceeds unchecked until too late. This process is what may make the "good times" such a bad time. They conceal a rot that can only be remedied at a dire price.

It is a telling exercise to read both Shirley Jackson's story and Kay Haugaard's essay and use them as yardsticks to measure where we stand today on several of the "first things" the American framers thought vital to a free society. Postmodern assaults on the framers and founders amount to a form of cultural terrorism. But as Lyman Beecher said to an earlier generation, the framers' example and standards "constitute a censorship inferior only to the eye of God; and to ridicule them is national suicide." Consider, for example, a trio of foundational concerns:

A nation "under God": If the framers' reliance on classical roots can be traced directly to thinkers such as Solon, Cicero, and Polybius, their debt to the Bible and the Jews is less specific but far more powerful. The nation is "under God" in the sense that it stands or falls in history under the moral judgment of God. Long before it became part of the Pledge of Allegiance, this theme, historically, was a weighty one. Thus Thomas Jefferson wrote of the evil of slavery, "I tremble for my country when I remember God is just." Congressman Davy Crockett said of his vote against Georgia's infamous forced removal of the Cherokee Indians in 1831, through which he lost his seat, "I gave a good honest vote, one that I believe will not make me ashamed on the day of judgment." And Abraham Lincoln solemnly recalled in his Second Inaugural Address that "the judgments of the Lord are true and righteous altogether."

Today neither national discourse nor popular religion betrays much evidence of living "under" anyone or anything, let alone God and moral judgment. The Ten Com-

117

mandments have been taken down not only from law courts and school walls but everyday life. Do we seriously believe that such a sea change has no consequences?

Character in leadership: John Adams—revolutionary, framer, and second president of the United States—spoke passionately of the importance of character. The American people, he wrote stunningly, "have a right, an indisputable, unalienable, indefeasible, divine right to that most dreaded and envied kind of knowledge—I mean of the character and conduct of their rulers." He was not alone. Thomas Jefferson wrote, "When a man assumes a public trust, he should consider himself as public property." Franklin Roosevelt said that "the Presidency is . . . preeminently a place of moral leadership." Peggy Noonan, speech writer for Ronald Reagan, concluded, "In a president, character is everything."

Today the consideration of character in leadership is all too often consigned to the private world or left in the public square only as a cliché or a weapon of attack. In political attack ads, for example, purported champions of character focus more attention on character assassination of their opponents than character celebration, and more on both than character formation. As the poet W. H. Auden noted, "One of the troubles of our times is that we are all, I think, precocious as personalities and backward as characters." Do we seriously believe such a sea change has no consequences?

The power of truth: "We hold these truths to be self-evident," Thomas Jefferson and his fellow revolutionaries declared of the primary tenets of American democracy. Or as Mr. Jefferson wrote elsewhere, quoting a traditional Irish saying, "Truth is great and shall prevail."

Today such sayings are "more a prayer than an axiom," one historian countered. Few things are less self-evident than truth. Truth, in fact, is said to be "dead"—or put more carefully, truth is relative, subjective, "socially constructed," and culturally determined; anything but objective, absolute, and universal. The result is politics by power plays in which "might makes right" and the one with the better lawyers, spinmeisters, muckrakers, and rumormongers wins. Do we seriously believe such a sea change has no consequences?

Is this concern for slow-motion cultural decline overblown? Is it only a luxury item compared to more urgent social issues? At the very least, the recent events reveal the fatuousness of reliance on "America's last public virtue"— responsibility. For when the classical virtues became no longer admissible in public, and even the virtue of tolerance was recognized as collapsing too easily into the vice of intolerance, the virtue of responsibility continued to be trumpeted unchallenged. Thus the Republican revolutionaries had a "Personal Responsibility Act" in their 1994 Contract with America, President Clinton put responsibility into his 1998 State of the Union address ("A strong nation rests on the rock of responsibility"), and countless American editorials still call loftily for "greater responsibility" as their catchall answer to numerous social ills.

It seems that few have stopped to ask why responsibility was not considered one of the classical virtues, though it clearly underlay them. Or to ask what responsibility means now that it is all "responsibility for" and no "responsibility to." The end result is the sorry spectacle of leaders trumpeting the virtue of responsibility while remaining mute when it comes to the response they owe the public.

There is a simple reason why slow-motion decline poses a particular threat to the American republic. Great civilizations and empires of the past have always been wrecked on two great reefs—the presence of sin in human society and the passing of time. No human success is forever.

The framers, of course, were keenly aware of both perils. The very audacity of what Washington called "the Great Experiment" and Lincoln "the undecided experiment" lay in its attempt to learn from history in order to defy history—and so to build a free society that would remain free. Their highest genius appears in the way they sought to avoid wreckage on the first reef through the separation of powers and an elaborate system of checks and balances. But they were powerless, as all human greatness is, to safeguard against the second. "This too shall pass away" allows for no exceptions.

Curiously, the year 1787 witnessed not only the "miracle" of the Constitutional Convention in Philadelphia but also the completion of the last volume of Edward Gibbon's *The History of the Decline and Fall of the Roman Empire*. A fall beyond belief, Rome's end—Gibbon wrote from Lausanne—was "the greatest, perhaps, and most awful scene in the history of mankind." And the first of the four reasons given? "The injuries of time and nature." In his Lyceum Address in 1837 Lincoln spoke similarly of "the silent artillery of time." As Gibbon explains, "The art of man is able to construct monuments far more permanent than the narrow span of his own existence: yet these monuments, like himself, are perishable and frail; and in the boundless annals of time his life and his labours must equally be measured as a fleeting moment."

I should make clear that I am not the slightest bit fatalistic or pessimistic about our situation today, though my reasons for confidence are irrelevant here. What is relevant is a striking paradox: Those who most ignore "the injury of time" lay themselves most open to its ravages, whereas those who best face that "this too shall pass away" best ensure that it will not happen in their time. In short, vigilance is a requirement for national renewal just as it is for freedom. If we are to avoid becoming accomplices in our own corruption and decline, current events and responses to them require watching and pondering.

A politics of charm is beguiling in the short term, but it only disguises the conditions and delays the consequences for a while. The good times will not roll forever and anyone who recognizes the raw Nietzschean will-to-power logic of recent political tactics must have shivered. Winter has just drawn closer, but citizens enjoying the Indian summer only yawned. To adopt Jesus' warning to his generation, "If these things have happened when the wood is green, what will it be like when the wood is dry?"

The Lottery

SHIRLEY JACKSON

The morning of June 27th was clear and sunny, with the fresh warmth of a full-summer day; the flowers were blossoming profusely and the grass was richly green. The people of the village began to gather in the square, between the post office and the bank, around ten o'clock; in some towns there were so many people that the lottery took two days and had to be started on June 26th, but in this village, where there were only about three hundred people, the whole lottery took less than two hours, so it could begin at ten o'clock in the morning and still be through in time to allow the villagers to get home for noon dinner.

The children assembled first, of course. School was recently over for the summer, and the feeling of liberty sat uneasily on most of them; they tended to gather together quietly for a while before they broke into boisterous play, and their talk was still of the classroom and the teacher, of books and reprimands. Bobby Martin had already stuffed his pockets full of stones, and the other boys soon followed his example, selecting the smoothest and roundest stones; Bobby and Harry Jones and Dickie Delacroix—the villagers pronounced this name "Delacroy"—eventually made a great pile of stones in one corner of the square and guarded it against the raids of the other boys. The girls stood aside, talking among themselves, looking over their shoulders at the boys, and the very small children rolled in the dust or clung to the hands of their older brothers or sisters.

Soon the men began to gather, surveying their own children, speaking of planting and rain, tractors and taxes. They stood together, away from the pile of stones in the corner, and their jokes were quiet and they smiled rather than laughed. The women, wearing faded house dresses and sweaters, came shortly after their menfolk. They greeted one another and exchanged bits of gossip as they went to join their husbands. Soon the women, standing by their husbands, began to call to their children, and the children came reluctantly, having to be called four or five times. Bobby Martin ducked under his mother's grasping hand and ran, laughing, back to the pile of stones. His father spoke up sharply, and Bobby came quickly and took his place between his father and his oldest brother.

The lottery was conducted—as were the square dances, the teen-age club, the Halloween program—by Mr. Summers, who had time and energy to devote to civic activities. He was a round-faced, jovial man and he ran the coal business, and people were sorry for him, because he had no children and his wife was a scold. When he arrived in the square, carrying the black wooden box, there was a murmur of conversation among the villagers, and he waved and called, "Little late today, folks." The postmaster, Mr. Graves, followed him, carrying a three-legged stool, and the stool was put in the center of the square and Mr. Summers set the black box down on it. The villagers kept their distance, leaving a space between themselves and the stool, and when Mr. Summers said, "Some of you fellows want to give me a hand?" there was a hesitation before two men, Mr. Martin and his oldest son, Baxter, came forward to hold the box steady on the stool while Mr. Summers stirred up the papers inside it.

The original paraphernalia for the lottery had been lost long ago, and the black box now resting on the stool had been put into use even before Old Man Warner, the oldest man in town, was born. Mr. Summers spoke frequently to the villagers about making a new box, but no one liked to upset even as much tradition as was represented by the black box. There was a story that the present box had been made with some pieces of the box that had preceded it, the one that had been constructed when the first people settled down to make a village here. Every year, after the lottery, Mr. Summers began talking again about a new box, but every year the subject was allowed to fade off without anything's being done. The black box grew shabbier each year; by now it was no longer completely black but splintered badly along one side to show the original wood color, and in some places faded or stained.

Mr. Martin and his oldest son, Baxter, held the black box securely on the stool until Mr. Summers had stirred the papers thoroughly with his hand. Because so much of the ritual had been forgotten or discarded, Mr. Summers had been successful in having slips of paper substituted for the chips of wood that had been used for generations. Chips of wood, Mr. Summers had argued, had been all very well when the village was tiny, but now that the population was more than three hundred and likely to keep on growing, it was necessary to use something that would fit more easily into the black box. The night before the lottery, Mr. Summers and Mr. Graves made up the slips of paper and put them in the box, and it was then taken to the safe of Mr. Summers' coal company and locked up until Mr. Summers was ready to take it to the square next morning. The rest of the year, the box was put away, sometimes one place, sometimes another; it had spent one year in Mr. Graves's barn and another year underfoot in the post office, and sometimes it was set on a shelf in the Martin grocery and left there.

There was a great deal of fussing to be done before Mr. Summers declared the lottery open. There were the lists to make up—of heads of families, heads of households in each family, members of each household in each family. There was the proper swearing-in of Mr. Summers by the post-master, as the official of the lottery; at one time, some people remembered, there had been a recital of some sort, performed by the official of the lottery, a perfunctory, tuneless chant that had been rattled off duly each year; some people believed that the official of the lottery used to stand just so when he said or sang it, others believed that he was supposed to walk among the people, but years and years ago this part of the ritual had been allowed to lapse. There had been, also, a ritual salute, which the official of the lottery had had to use in addressing each person who came up to draw from the box, but this also had changed with time, until now it was felt necessary only for the official to speak to each person approaching. Mr. Summers was very good at all this; in his clean white shirt and blue jeans, with one hand resting carelessly on the black box, he seemed very proper and important as he talked interminably to Mr. Graves and the Martins.

Just as Mr. Summers finally left off talking and turned to the assembled villagers, Mrs. Hutchinson came hurriedly along the path to the square, her sweater thrown over her shoulders, and slid into place in the back of the crowd. "Clean forgot what day it was," she said to Mrs. Delacroix, who stood next to her, and they both laughed softly. "Thought my old man was out back stacking wood," Mrs. Hutchinson went on, "and then I looked out the window and the kids were gone, and then I remembered it was the

126

twenty-seventh and came a-running." She dried her hands on her apron, and Mrs. Delacroix said, "You're in time, though. They're still talking away up there."

Mrs. Hutchinson craned her neck to see through the crowd and found her husband and children standing near the front. She tapped Mrs. Delacroix on the arm as a farewell and began to make her way through the crowd. The people separated good-humoredly to let her through; two or three people said, in voices just loud enough to be heard across the crowd, "Here comes your Missus Hutchinson," and "Bill, she made it after all." Mrs. Hutchinson reached her husband, and Mr. Summers, who had been waiting, said cheerfully, "Thought we were going to have to get on without you, Tessie." Mrs. Hutchinson said grinning, "Wouldn't have me leave m'dishes in the sink, now, would you, Joe?" and soft laughter ran through the crowd as the people stirred back into position after Mrs. Hutchinson's arrival.

"Well, now," Mr. Summers said soberly, "guess we better get started, get this over with, so's we can go back to work. Anybody ain't here?"

"Dunbar," several people said. "Dunbar, Dunbar."

Mr. Summers consulted his list. "Clyde Dunbar," he said. "That's right. He's broke his leg, hasn't he? Who's drawing for him?"

"Me, I guess," a woman said, and Mr. Summers turned to look at her. "Wife draws for her husband," Mr. Summers said. "Don't you have a grown boy to do it for you, Janey?" Although Mr. Summers and everyone else in the village knew the answer perfectly well, it was the business of the official of the lottery to ask such questions formally. Mr. Summers waited with an expression of polite interest while Mrs. Dunbar answered.

"Horace's not but sixteen yet," Mrs. Dunbar said regretfully. "Guess I gotta fill in for the old man this year."

127

"Right," Mr. Summers said. He made a note on the list he was holding. Then he asked, "Watson boy drawing this year?"

A tall boy in the crowd raised his hand. "Here," he said. "I'm drawing for m'mother and me." He blinked his eyes nervously and ducked his head as several voices in the crowd said things like "Good fellow, Jack," and "Glad to see your mother's got a man to do it."

"Well," Mr. Summers said, "guess that's everyone. Old Man Warner make it?"

"Here," a voice said, and Mr. Summers nodded.

A sudden hush fell on the crowd as Mr. Summers cleared his throat and looked at the list. "All ready?" he called. "Now, I'll read the names—heads of families first—and the men come up and take a paper out of the box. Keep the paper folded in your hand without looking at it until everyone has had a turn. Everything clear?"

The people had done it so many times that they only half listened to the directions, most of them were quiet, wetting their lips, not looking around. Then Mr. Summers raised one hand high and said, "Adams." A man disengaged himself from the crowd and came forward. "Hi, Steve," Mr. Summers said, and Mr. Adams said, "Hi, Joe." They grinned at one another humorlessly and nervously. Then Mr. Adams reached into the black box and took out a folded paper. He held it firmly by one corner as he turned and went hastily back to his place in the crowd, where he stood a little apart from his family, not looking down at his hand.

"Allen," Mr. Summers said. "Anderson . . . Bentham."

"Seems like there's no time at all between lotteries any more," Mrs. Delacroix said to Mrs. Graves in the back row. "Seems like we got through with the last one only last week."

"Time sure goes fast," Mrs. Graves said.

"Clark . . . Delacroix."

"There goes my old man," Mrs. Delacroix said. She held her breath while her husband went forward.

"Dunbar," Mr. Summers said, and Mrs. Dunbar went steadily to the box while one of the women said, "Go on, Janey," and another said, "There she goes."

"We're next," Mrs. Graves said. She watched while Mr. Graves came around from the side of the box, greeted Mr. Summers gravely, and selected a slip of paper from the box. By now, all through the crowd there were men holding the small folded papers in their large hands, turning them over and over nervously. Mrs. Dunbar and her two sons stood together, Mrs. Dunbar holding the slip of paper.

"Harburt . . . Hutchinson."

"Get up there, Bill," Mrs. Hutchinson said, and the people near her laughed.

"Jones."

"They do say," Mr. Adams said to Old Man Warner, who stood next to him, "that over in the north village they're talking of giving up the lottery."

Old Man Warner snorted. "Pack of crazy fools," he said. "Listening to the young folks, nothing's good enough for them. Next thing you know, they'll be wanting to go back to living in caves, nobody work any more, live that way for a while. Used to be a saying about 'Lottery in June, corn be heavy soon.' First thing you know, we'd all be eating stewed chickweed and acorns. There's always been a lottery," he added petulantly. "Bad enough to see young Joe Summers up there joking with everybody."

"Some places have already quit lotteries," Mrs. Adams said.

"Nothing but trouble in that," Old Man Warner said stoutly. "Pack of young fools."

"Martin." And Bobby Martin watched his father go forward. "Overdyke . . . Percy."

"I wish they'd hurry," Mrs. Dunbar said to her older son. "I wish they'd hurry."

"They're almost through," her son said.

"You get ready to run tell Dad," Mrs. Dunbar said.

Mr. Summers called his own name and then stepped forward precisely and selected a slip from the box. Then he called, "Warner."

"Seventy-seventh year I been in the lottery," Old Man Warner said as he went through the crowd. "Seventy-seventh time."

"Watson." The tall boy came awkwardly through the crowd. Someone said, "Don't be nervous, Jack," and Mr. Summers said, "Take your time, son."

"Zanini."

After that, there was a long pause, a breathless pause until Mr. Summers, holding his slip of paper in the air, said, "All right fellows." For a minute, no one moved, and then all the slips of paper were opened. Suddenly, all the women began to speak at once, saying "Who is it?" "Who's got it?" "Is it the Dunbars?" "Bill Hutchinson's got it."

"Go tell your father," Mrs. Dunbar said to her older son.

People began to look around to see the Hutchinsons. Bill Hutchinson was standing quiet, staring down at the paper in his hand. Suddenly, Tessie Hutchinson shouted to Mr. Summers, "You didn't give him time enough to take any paper he wanted. I saw you. It wasn't fair."

"Be a good sport, Tessie." Mrs. Delacroix called, and Mrs. Graves said, "All of us took the same chance."

"Shut up, Tessie," Bill Hutchinson said.

"Well, everyone," Mr. Summers said, "That was done pretty fast, and now we've got to be hurrying a little more to get done in time." He consulted his next list. "Bill, you draw for the Hutchinson family. You got any other households in the Hutchinsons?"

"There's Don and Eva," Mrs. Hutchinson yelled. "Make them take their chance!"

"Daughters draw with their husband's families, Tessie," Mr. Summers said gently. "You know that as well as anyone else."

"It wasn't fair," Tessie said.

"I guess not, Joe," Bill Hutchinson said regretfully. "My daughter draws with her husband's family, that's only fair. And I've got no other family except the kids."

"Then, as far as drawing for families is concerned it's you," Mr. Summers said in explanation, "and as far as drawing for households is concerned, that's you, too. Right?"

"Right," Bill Hutchinson said.

"How many kids, Bill?" Mr. Summers asked formally.

"Three," Bill Hutchinson said. "There's Bill, Jr., and Nancy, and little Dave. And Tessie and me."

"All right, then," Mr. Summers said. "Harry, you got their tickets back?"

Mr. Graves nodded and held up the slips of paper. "Put them in the box, then," Mr. Summers directed. "Take Bill's and put it in."

"I think we ought to start over," Mrs. Hutchinson said, as quietly as she could. "I tell you it wasn't fair. You didn't give him time enough to choose. Everybody saw that."

Mr. Graves had selected the five slips and put them in the box, and he dropped all the papers but those onto the ground, where the breeze caught them and lifted them off.

"Listen, everybody," Mrs. Hutchinson was saying to the people around her.

"Ready, Bill?" Mr. Summers asked, and Bill Hutchinson, with one quick glance around at his wife and children, nodded.

"Remember," Mr. Summers said, "take the slips and keep them folded until each person has taken one. Harry, you help little Dave." Mr. Graves took the hand of the little boy, who came willingly with him up to the box. "Take a paper out of the box, Davy," Mr. Summers said. Davy put his hand into the box and laughed. "Take just one paper," Mr. Summers said. "Harry, you hold it for him." Mr. Graves took the child's hand and removed the folded paper from the tight fist and held it while little Dave stood next to him and looked up at him wonderingly.

"Nancy next," Mr. Summers said. Nancy was twelve, and her school friends breathed heavily as she went forward, switching her skirt, and took a slip daintily from the box. "Bill, Jr.," Mr. Summers said, and Billy, his face red and his feet over-large, nearly knocked the box over as he got a paper out. "Tessie," Mr. Summers said. She hesitated for a minute, looking around defiantly, and then set her lips and went up to the box. She snatched a paper out and held it behind her.

"Bill," Mr. Summers said, and Bill Hutchinson reached into the box and felt around, bringing his hand out at last with the slip of paper in it.

The crowd was quiet. A girl whispered, "I hope it's not Nancy," and the sound of the whisper reached the edges of the crowd.

"It's not the way it used to be," Old Man Warner said clearly. "People ain't the way they used to be."

"All right," Mr. Summers said. "Open the papers. Harry, you open little Dave's."

Mr. Graves opened the slip of paper and there was a general sigh through the crowd as he held it up and everyone could see that it was blank. Nancy and Bill, Jr., opened theirs at the same time, and both beamed and laughed, turning around to the crowd and holding their slips of paper above their heads.

"Tessie," Mr. Summers said. There was a pause, and then Mr. Summers looked at Bill Hutchinson, and Bill unfolded his paper and showed it. It was blank.

"It's Tessie," Mr. Summers said, and his voice was hushed. "Show us her paper, Bill."

Bill Hutchinson went over to his wife and forced the slip of paper out of her hand. It had a black spot on it, the black spot Mr. Summers had made the night before with the heavy pencil in the coal-company office. Bill Hutchinson held it up, and there was a stir in the crowd.

"All right, folks," Mr. Summers said. "Let's finish quickly."

Although the villagers had forgotten the ritual and lost the original black box, they still remembered to use stones. The pile of stones the boys had made earlier was ready; there were stones on the ground with the blowing scraps of paper that had come out of the box. Mrs. Delacroix selected a stone so large she had to pick it up with both hands and turned to Mrs. Dunbar. "Come on," she said. "Hurry up."

Mrs. Dunbar had small stones in both hands, and she said, gasping for breath, "I can't run at all. You'll have to go ahead and I'll catch up with you."

The children had stones already, and someone gave little Davy Hutchinson a few pebbles.

Tessie Hutchinson was in the center of a cleared space by now, and she held her hands out desperately as the villagers moved in on her. "It isn't fair," she said. A stone hit her on the side of the head.

Old Man Warner was saying, "Come on, come on, everyone." Steve Adams was in the front of the crowd of villagers, with Mrs. Graves beside him.

"It isn't fair, it isn't right," Mrs. Hutchinson screamed, and then they were upon her.

The Lottery Revisited

KAY HAUGAARD

Once again I was going to teach Shirley Jackson's short story "The Lottery." I sighed as I gathered my books to leave for my evening class in creative writing; I had taught this story so many times over the past two decades.

Not that "The Lottery" wasn't an excellent story. On the contrary, it was masterful and stunning, well deserving of its long-held position in almost every literary anthology.

Each week during the semester, I allowed a student to select a story from an anthology for the class to read and then discuss at the next session. Throughout the twenty-four years that I had been teaching creative writing, I had found that the various anthologies that I had used, as well as the stories written by the students themselves during the semester, had reflected national changes in social mores and attitudes.

When I started teaching, in 1970, my students—ranging from an occasional eighteen-year-old to an occasional eighty-year-old—were still shocked into giggles or frowns at the sound of naughty words, whether they appeared in the published stories we read or in students' work. The youngest students (mostly the males) wrote pieces calculated to shock and reveled in an abundant use of vulgar slang and details of drug parties and sexual encounters. Remembering my commitment to freedom of speech, I steeled myself and read all of the students' stories out loud to the class, even when I could feel my cheeks flaming.

A few years later, I started getting floods of powerful stories written by Vietnam veterans, who described killing, maiming, being wounded and crippled, having friends die in their laps, and sexual encounters with Vietnamese prostitutes.

As the years went by, the students seemed to become jaded by obscenities. If a story contained a great deal of lewdness, they sighed and pointed out that it was boringly excessive. The Vietnam War began to fade and, for the first time, we began reading students' narratives of homosexual inclinations and encounters. At first these, too, startled the class. The students did not condemn the stories, but their eyes flew open in visible shock. A student would say, "Did I understand it right? The characters were two men, not a man and a woman?" Assured that that interpretation was correct, the student usually did not respond, but sat back with a serious, reflective expression.

Several years later, narratives of lesbianism began to enter the work I received. Some students described themselves as "radical feminists" and wrote of same-sex love affairs. One young woman wrote of two lesbians living together as a married couple. One of the characters became artificially impregnated by the other one's brother and gave birth. Once again, this startled the students and they sat back, not in condemnation, but in ruminative silence. It seemed as though events and changing attitudes in the world outside the classroom had prepared them to accept

136

previously forbidden actions in the material their fellow students wrote. Or perhaps they did not feel comfortable expressing opposition in public.

Along with the students' stories, anthology after anthology mirrored the social concerns of the particular period in which it was published: free speech issues, civil rights, sexual liberation, feminism, and, most recently, multiculturalism. But every anthology, without fail, included "The Lottery," and students often chose the story for discussion.

Although I had escaped the story for a couple of years, as I left for class I rather wearily went over in my mind the students' inevitable responses, ones that I had heard as many times as the story had been discussed in class.

The story opens with a depiction of the residents of an American country village. It is a brilliant summer morning, and people are gathering for some kind of amoral ritual. The people are portrayed as warm, loving, hardworking, and earnest; they pique our curiosity by mentioning, but not describing, a lottery that is important to the crops. Mr. Adams starts to say that some villages have stopped the lotteries, but Old Man Warner cuts off all further discussion by declaring those people a "pack of young fools."

We get to know one family—the Hutchinsons. Tess Hutchinson, the mother, arrives late for the public drawing, explaining that she had to do the dishes. Her twelve-year-old daughter talks with friends; her little son, Dave, gathers a pile of stones—the sort of thing little boys play at. According to the custom, Tess's husband draws a ticket for the whole family from a black box. Nothing prepares the first-time reader for what happens next: Everyone, including four-year-old Dave, sets on Tess Hutchinson and stones her to death. This is a lottery for human sacrifice.

Students who had never read this story were always absolutely stunned by it—as though they personally had been struck with the first ritual stone. I had vivid mental pictures of their faces as we discussed the story: wide-eyed, unsmiling, disturbed. They made comments such as, "I thought this was kind of an ordinary little story, and then wham! I never thought . . ."

Students who had read the story before were calmer but admitted that it had shocked them the first time. Everyone thought it was scary because, as someone inevitably said, "The characters seem just like regular people—you know, like us!"

The story always impressed the class with the insight that I felt the author had intended: the danger of just "going along" with something habitually, without examining its rationale and value. The power of public pressure was illustrated chillingly, in the ease with which the conversation about other villages dropping the practice had been squelched.

In spite of the changes that I had witnessed over the years in anthologies and in students' writing, Jackson's message about blind conformity always spoke to my students' sense of right and wrong. Jackson had made an important and powerful point, which I hoped my students would take to heart, becoming more analytical about why things are done as they are.

That evening, I thought to myself, it would be more fun if we had a story to discuss that I had not read before.

"So, what did you think of 'The Lottery'?" I asked as soon as I sat down in front of the class.

Beth, a slender, stylish woman in her mid-forties, pushed up the sleeves of her enormously baggy sweater as she spoke: "I was rather surprised that this seemed to be taking place in the United States and like it was right now."

"Yes, it does make it more shocking when the characters seem like people we might know, or even be, doesn't it?" I said. "How about you, Jeanette?" I asked the plump nineteen-year-old, whose dyed black ringlets framed an ivory, Kewpie-doll face.

She replied: "It was pretty boring until the end. The end was neat!"

"Neat?" I asked, "How do mean, neat?"

"Just neat! I liked it."

"I see. Kind of Stephen King 'neat,' I suppose." I turned to Edward, well dressed in the suit he had worn to his job as a high school teacher that day. "What was your response to the story, Edward?"

He bounced the foot of his crossed leg and looked up with a kind of bored expression. "It was all right. It wasn't that great."

But, I pressed, "How about that ending, where the whole village turns on one of their neighbors and kills her with stones? Had you read it before?"

Edward furrowed his brow but refused to be impressed. "No, I hadn't read it before. It was all right."

I could not believe these responses. Everyone seemed so blasé. Giving up on Edward, who was never very vocal in discussions, I turned to Richard, a slightly graying elementary school teacher. "Why do these people perform this ritual, Richard, this human sacrifice?"

He took a deep breath. "Well, I agree with Beth that it was pretty surprising to have it take place right today, as it were."

"But why do they do it?" I persisted.

"Uh, well, it isn't too clear."

Someone else spoke up. "For the crops. They do it so the crops will grow well."

"That's one of the reasons they give," I responded, pleased that someone had found a clue in the text. "Is that a sufficient justification? Any other reason?"

"They just always do it. It's a ritual," said Maria.

"That's right. They do it because they've always done it," I said.

"I was wondering if there was anything religious about it," said Beth. "If this were part of something of long standing. It doesn't seem to be religious."

"Would that make a difference, if it were part of a religious ritual?"

Beth furrowed her brows and gazed toward the ceiling.

"There isn't anything mentioned in the story about religion, but it does seem related to religious traditions of human sacrifice intended to make the crops grow better," I said. I took a few moments to talk about Sir James Frazer's "The Golden Bough," which describes many cultures with such traditions.

"Oh, well, if it was something like that . . . ," Beth responded.

"How do you mean? That would make it all right?"

"Are you asking me if I believe in human sacrifice?" Beth responded thoughtfully, as though seriously considering all aspects of the question.

"Well, yes," I managed to say. "Do you think that the author approved or disapproved of this ritual?" I was stunned: This was the woman who wrote so passionately of saving the whales, of concern for the rain forests, of her rescue and tender care of a stray dog.

"I really don't know. If it was a religion of long standing . . ."

For a moment I couldn't even respond. This woman actually couldn't seem to bring herself to say plainly that she was against human sacrifice. My classes of a few years before would have burst into nervous giggles at the suggestion. This class was calmly considering it.

"There have been studies," said Richard, "about certain cultures, and they show that, when there aren't any killings for a long time, the people seem to . . . require it to satisfy this . . ."

I listened in a state of shock as Richard went on to describe a psychological theory he had read that seemed to espouse the social function of a certain amount of bloodshed. "It almost seems a need," he concluded in cool, reasonable tones.

140

It was too much. I had always tried to keep my personal feelings out of class discussion and allow the students to discover a story's theme and significance as much as possible. But I had reached my limit.

"There certainly are precedents for it," I said, "but does a precedent necessarily make something right? I think the author strongly disapproves of this ritual and is attempting to shock us into reexamining our activities every now and then to see if they still seem justified and functional."

I went on, probably longer than I should have. "The Aztecs believed that the sun would not rise if they did not feed the hummingbird god Huichtlipochtli with human blood. This was their rationale for human sacrifice. But we know that the sun will rise on its own. Are these things justified on the basis of precedent?"

I turned to Patricia, a fifty-something, red-headed nurse. She had always seemed an intelligent person of moderate views.

"Well, I teach a course for our hospital personnel in multicultural understanding, and if it is part of a person's culture, we are taught not to judge, and if it has worked for them . . ."

At this point I gave up. No one in the whole class of more than twenty ostensibly intelligent individuals would go out on a limb and take a stand against human sacrifice.

I wound up the discussion. "Frankly, I feel it's clear that the author was pointing out the dangers of being totally accepting followers, too cowardly to rebel against obvious cruelties and injustices." I was shaken, and I thought that the author, whose story had shocked so many, would have been shaken as well.

The class finally ended. It was a warm night when I walked out to my car after class that evening, but I felt shivery, chilled to the bone.

Os Guinness is an author of numerous books and a speaker of international renown. Born in China and educated in England, he is a graduate of Oxford University. Dr. Guinness has lived in the United States since 1984 and has been a visiting fellow at the Brookings Institution. He is currently senior fellow of The Trinity Forum, a "leadership academy without walls" that engages the leading ideas of our day in the context of faith. He resides in McLean, Virginia.